Executive Skills

Philip Minkoff

Prentice Hall

New York   London   Toronto   Sydney   Tokyo   Singapore

PRENTICE HALL INTERNATIONAL ENGLISH LANGUAGE

Other ESP titles of interest include:

Adamson, D.
Starting English for Business ⋆

Business Management English Series:
Brieger, N. and J. Comfort
Production and Operations ⋆

Brieger, N. and J. Comfort
Personnel ⋆

Comfort, J. and N. Brieger
Marketing ⋆

Comfort, J. and N. Brieger
Finance ⋆

Brieger, N. and J. Comfort
Language Reference for Business English

Brieger, N. and J. Comfort
Early Business Contacts

Brieger, N. and J. Comfort
Developing Business Contacts ⋆

Brieger, N. and J. Comfort
Advanced Business Contacts ⋆

Brieger, N. and A. Cornish
Secretarial Contacts ⋆

Brieger, N. and J. Comfort
Technical Contacts ⋆

Brieger, N. and J. Comfort
Social Contacts ⋆

Brieger, N. and J. Comfort
Business Issues

Brieger, N. and S. Sweeney
The Language of Business English

Davies, S. *et al.*
*Bilingual Handbook of Business
Correspondence and Communication*

Goddard, C.
Business Idioms International ⋆

Sneyd, M.
International Banking and Finance ⋆
Accounting ⋆
Insurance ⋆

⋆ Includes audio cassette(s)

First published 1994 by
Prentice Hall International (UK) Ltd
Campus 400, Maylands Avenue
Hemel Hempstead
Hertfordshire, HP2 7EZ
A division of
Simon & Schuster International Group

Typeset in 9/12pt Plantin
by PanTek Arts, Maidstone, Kent.

Printed and bound in Great Britain by Redwood Books, Trowbridge

Library of Congress Cataloging-in-Publication Data

Minkoff, Philip.
Executive skills/Philip Minkoff.
p. cm. — (English language teaching)
ISBN 0-13-017781-4
1. English language — Business English. 2. Business communication.
I. Title. II. Series: English language teaching (Englewood Cliffs, N.J.)
PE1115.M535 1993
808' .06665—dc20   93-30936 CIP

British Library Cataloguing in Publication Data

A catalogue record for this book is available from the British Library

ISBN 0-13-017781-4

4 5 98 97 96 95

Contents

Acknowledgments

I am grateful to the following for permission to reproduce copyright material: British Petroleum (page 40), Guinness (page 85) and Merrill Lynch (page 125) for extracts from their annual reports; McGraw Hill for 5 extracts from *Business Today* by David J Rachman and Michael H Mescon; the Commodities Exchange Center Inc, New York, for the script on the visitors' gallery at the CEC (page 148); *The Economist* for an extract from the article *Discounting for Creativity* (page 117); Pelican Publications for an extract from *An Insight into Management Accounting* by John Sizer (page 118); *The Financial Times* for the table of pay (page 39); Neilson for the tables and graphs in Unit 6.

I would also like to thank my colleagues at the Nantes Graduate School of Management, France, for their valuable advice and support. I wish to thank, in particular, Danièle Bouder Pailler, Christopher DeMarco, Aïssa Dermouche, Michel Fonchain, Alain Gourvest and Jacques Hermant. I am particularly indebted to Caroline Gilbert for helping me prepare the manuscripts.

Special thanks to Professor Randolph Bobbitt at the Ohio State University for his help with the sections on management, to Bill Howell for his invaluable advice on the accounting documents, to Will Capel for his constructive criticism and to all the teachers and students involved in piloting the material.

Finally, thanks to Martine for everything.

Introduction

Who is this book for?

Executive Skills is a communication skills book for upper intermediate and advanced learners of business English. It aims at people who have, or who will have, managerial responsibilities, and is suitable for both pre-work students and professionals with business and management experience.

The book may be successfully used by the following:

- undergraduate students in business schools
- undergraduate and graduate students in non-business disciplines (eg communications, engineering or any field of scientific research) who will soon be working in a company and need to understand the main management concepts and develop the skills required for professional life
- small, mixed groups of sales personnel, management trainees, senior supervisors, junior, middle and senior managers, product managers, and public relations officers taking part in ESP programmes.

What does the book contain?

The book covers the three main functional areas of management: Human Resources, Marketing, and Finance. Each of these areas is broken down into three units which deal with a major concern of the management area. The units, in turn, are broken down into sections that concentrate on a topic area. Each unit presents a variety of activities which include the presentation and development of key terms and concepts, discussions, case studies, analysis of data, language development tasks and group projects.

The book also develops the communication skills which managers and future managers need. These include:

- negotiating
- using the telephone
- summarising
- public speaking
- presenting information visually
- writing reports, letters, and CVs.

How can the book be used?

The emphasis throughout is on interaction. As such, the activities work best with groups, though many of them can be used in a one-to-one teaching situation. *Executive Skills* should be considered as a main coursebook, to be used alone or in conjunction with a general English coursebook if more intensive study is required. The material is best used sequentially, since some activities provide input for subsequent ones. There is still room for considerable flexibility, however, and teachers wishing to supplement other course books will find here a rich bank of resources.

To Martine

PART I
Human Resources

Recruitment

Recruitment sources

1.1.A
Warm-up

Finding a job

Work in groups. You have just met some people who would like to work in your country. What advice can you give them about current job prospects and how to go about finding a job? The following headings may help you:

- availability of jobs in different industries
- availability of jobs geographically
- employment sources (newspapers, agencies, etc)
- part-time/full-time work
- blue collar/white collar jobs
- seasonal work.

1.1.B
Reading

Recruitment

Read the following extract from a recruitment handbook and answer the questions which follow it.

There are many ways in which an organisation can recruit personnel. Posting a list of vacancies on the company noticeboard or publishing it in employee magazines is fairly common and gives current employees the opportunity of applying for a position. Similarly, a subordinate may be referred for a position by his or her superior.

Another means of recruiting internally is to search in the organisation's existing files. Some companies have a data base of their employees' skills and special interests. Reviewing these files periodically may reveal employees who are well-suited to a particular position.

Although recruiting people within the organisation can have many advantages, it does have its limitations. If companies wish to be dynamic it is essential to inject new blood from time to time. Similarly, existing employees may not have the necessary skills that the position requires. Consequently, it is often necessary to recruit people from outside the organisation.

Advertising is a commonly used technique for recruiting people from outside. The advertising medium should be chosen according to the type of public the organisation is aiming at. If a highly specialised person is required, a speciality publication such as a trade magazine may be most appropriate. National newspapers and magazines sometimes carry a *Senior Appointments* section for specialised personnel. Many national and local newspapers have a *General Appointments* section, or a *Classified Ads* section for less specialised personnel. Radio and television advertising of vacancies is relatively underdeveloped in most countries.

Employment agencies may be another source of recruitment. State-backed agencies compete with private agencies in many countries. In general, private agencies charge a fee whereas public sector agencies offer their services free of charge. Another difference is that private agencies tend to offer more specific services; for example, they may specialise in a particular area of recruitment such as temporary secretaries, middle managers or senior executives. They may also include search services, otherwise known as headhunting, or provide management consulting.

Current employees are sometimes encouraged to refer friends, family and ex-colleagues to fill a particular vacancy. This is particularly true in occupations such as nursing where there is a shortage of trained people.

Other valuable sources of recruitment may be university campuses, trade unions, professional organisations and unsolicited applications.

1 List all the forms of internal recruitment mentioned in the passage.

2 Why do companies often recruit from outside the organisation?

3 Which kinds of organisations are most likely to recruit through referrals by existing employees?

Explaining key terms

Write a sentence explaining what each of the following words mean as they are used in the above passage.

posting	data base
vacancies	fee
subordinate	headhunting
files	unsolicited applications

Pros and cons of recruitment sources

Work in small groups. Choose four of the following recruitment sources and discuss what you think are the advantages and disadvantages of each from the recruiter's point of view. When you have finished your discussion, report back to the rest of the class.

- publishing vacancies in the company magazine
- keeping a data base/files
- advertising in speciality publications
- advertising in the national or regional press
- radio and television advertising
- employment agencies (public and private)
- unsolicited applications.

Recruitment sources

Table 1 is part of a study into the effectiveness of different recruitment sources in six American states. The figures are based on a sample of 100 companies. They represent the successful recruitment over the past five years of five employee groups according to recruitment source.

Look at Table 1 and answer the questions which follow it.

Table 1:
The effectiveness of different recruitment sources

Recruitment source	Occupation				
	Office/ clerical	Plant/ service	Sales	Professional/ technical	Management
Company noticeboards	12	15	5	1	0
In-house magazine	8	7	4	2	0
Data base/files	7	3	2	1	8
Speciality publications	0	0	3	5	8
National/regional press	31	23	28	30	26
Radio and television	0	1	0	1	0
Public employment agencies	7	14	2	8	0
Private employment agencies	8	2	25	15	25
Referrals from current employees	14	15	10	6	5
Campuses	1	3	8	10	6
Unions	0	2	0	1	0
Professional organisations	0	1	1	2	4
Unsolicited applications	12	14	8	10	1
Search firms	0	0	4	8	17
Total	100	100	100	100	100

1 What are the most effective recruitment sources?

2 How could a Personnel Manager use this information?

1.1.F
Word choice

Comparisons and superlatives

Fill in the gaps in the following sentences using the information from Table 1.

1 Company noticeboards are used _____
often _____ public employment agencies for
recruiting clerical staff.

2 Almost as _____ clerical staff
_____ service staff are recruited through
referrals.

3 Radio and television are the _____
_____ recruiting media for almost all
occupations.

4 _____ more clerical workers are recruited
through referrals from current employees _____
through company noticeboards.

5 Television and radio are the _____ effective
recruiting sources of all.

6 Managers are recruited _____ through the
press and agencies.

7 _____   _____
half _____ all sales personnel are recruited
through the press and private employment agencies.

8 Professional organisations are a relatively _____
source for most occupations.

9 In-house magazines recruit _____
_____ plant/service personnel than office/
clerical staff.

10 Public employment agencies recruit _____
_____ many plant/service workers as
office/clerical workers.

11 _____   _____
many professional/technical personnel are recruited through private employment agencies _____ through the press.

12 Overall, the national and regional press recruit more than eight
_____ as _____
people as do speciality publications.

Section 2

Job descriptions

1.2.A
Vocabulary

Who does what?

Place each of the following words into the grid below.

PR officer	book-keeper	clerk	shorthand typist
Managing Director/CEO	unskilled worker	skil' d worker	foreman
fundraiser	PA	systems analyst	data base administrator

What (s)he does	Who (s)he is
1 Does manual work which requires a certain level of trained ability.	
2 Keeps an accurate record of the company's transactions (sales, purchases, loans, wage payments, etc).	
3 Has wider responsibilities than those of a secretary and may perform part of his or her superior's duties.	
4 Is in charge of the way a company is run.	
5 Is responsible for storing readily accessible information on the company's computer system.	
6 Collects money to support a charity, political campaign, organisation, etc.	
7 Works in an office or bank and looks after the records.	
8 Does work that does not require any special training.	
9 Writes down what somebody dictates and then types it up.	
10 Deals with the company's internal and external communication.	
11 Is in charge of a group of workers.	
12 Plans the company's computer requirements and supervises the programmers.	

Project

Choosing an appropriate recruitment source

1 You are in charge of recruiting personnel. Choose one of the positions and one of the organisations listed below. In each case write a job description and decide on the most appropriate recruitment source. Give a reason for choosing this source.

Example

> **Organisation:** well established American leisure group
> **Position:** business/finance analyst
> **Job description:** to assist the Information Systems (IS) co-ordinator in the support and installation of a number of accountancy systems running multi-currency, multi-lingual and multi-company accounts throughout Europe
> **Recruitment source:** advertisement in national press under *Appointments in Computing Science and Technology*
> **Reason:** Although this position requires specialist skills, the general press should be adequate. The company's personnel department can screen and select applicants without having to use the services of a specialist agency.

Positions:

- PR officer
- financial controller
- shopfloor foreman
- accountant
- Senior Internal Auditor
- printer
- shorthand typist
- systems analyst

- librarian
- unskilled worker
- business/finance analyst
- product manager
- skilled worker
- book-keeper
- PA to Marketing Director
- undergraduate trainee

- clerk
- electrical engineer
- graphic designer
- Managing Director/CEO
- data base administrator
- fundraising manager
- semi-skilled worker

Organisations:

- a large state university
- a car showroom
- a foreign based subsidiary of a well-established British manufacturer
- an international airport
- a national environment-protection group
- the head office of a regional supermarket chain

- a clothing shop
- a recently launched record company
- a merchant bank
- an electronic components manufacturer
- a large construction company
- an American multinational
- a well-established American leisure group

2 Work in small groups. One student presents the organisation and position he has chosen, and reads the job description *but not the source*. The other students discuss which source would be most appropriate and why. The presenter reveals his source and justifies his decision in the event of any disagreement.

Section 3

Applying for a job

Vocabulary

Action verbs

Action verbs are used by both recruiter and job applicant, and play a prominent role in job descriptions, CVs, and letters of application.

Choose an appropriate heading from the list below for each of the following nine groups of verbs.

creative skills	research skills	management skills
clerical skills	financial skills	teaching skills
helping skills	technical skills	communication skills

1 assign
attain
chair
co-ordinate
delegate
direct
execute
increase
organise
oversee
plan
produce
recommend
review
strengthen
supervise

2 address
arbitrate
arrange
correspond
draft
edit
lecture
mediate
motivate
negotiate
persuade
publicise
reconcile
recruit
speak
translate
write

3 collect
critique
diagnose
evaluate
examine
extract
identify
interpret
investigate
summarise
survey

4 assemble
build
calculate
devise
engineer
fabricate
maintain
operate
overhaul
programme
remodel
repair
solve
upgrade

5 advise
clarify
coach
enable
encourage
explain
inform
initiate
instruct
persuade
set goals
stimulate
train

6 administer
allocate
analyse
appraise
audit
balance
budget
compute
develop
forecast
project

7 conceptualise
create
design
fashion
illustrate
institute
integrate
invent
perform
revitalise
shape

8 assess
assist
counsel
demonstrate
diagnose
facilitate
guide
refer
rehabilitate
represent

9 catalogue
classify
compile
dispatch
generate
implement
monitor
process
record
retrieve
specify
tabulate
validate

Verbs and nouns in context

I.3.B
Vocabulary

I Match the phrases on the left with those on the right to make full sentences.

1 She assigned us ...	**a** the team next season.
2 He attained ...	**b** the report immediately.
3 She chaired ...	**c** an impossible task.
4 I'll draft ...	**d** our archaic accounting system.
5 We need to overhaul ...	**e** new products for the 21st century.
6 We should upgrade ...	**f** sales for next year.
7 Jack will be coaching ...	**g** the meeting brilliantly.
8 It's difficult to forecast ...	**h** his lifelong ambition.
9 We need to devise ...	**i** her job from secretary to PA.

2 Make a list of the nouns which correspond to the following verbs.

Example

> to assist → assistance

1	to administer	12	to arrange
2	to analyse	13	to draft
3	to assign	14	to speak
4	to attain	15	to diagnose
5	to develop	16	to evaluate
6	to execute	17	to assemble
7	to improve	18	to build
8	to increase	19	to solve
9	to recommend	20	to train
10	to strengthen	21	to advise
11	to supervise	22	to encourage

Examine the noun endings. Which ones appear most frequently?

3 Fill in the blanks in the following paragraph using your list of nouns from the exercise above.

The first _____1_____ of Bill's script was full of inaccuracies and had to be completely rewritten, but public speaking was never his main _____2_____ . The _____3_____ he made at the AGM was mostly dull but he did mention that the next _____4_____ would take place just after Christmas. By that time, my overseas _____5_____ will be well under way. Bill's been giving me a lot of _____6*_____ and seems fairly optimistic that we'll come up with a(n) _____7_____ to the deadlock in Korea. I think two of the keys are better _____8_____ and closer _____9_____ of the production personnel, which should, hopefully, lead to a vast _____10_____ in quality.

*two possibilities

1.3.C
Writing

The letter of application/cover letter: layout

When applying for a job, you should send a letter of application. It should state:

● why you are writing
● where you learned about the position
● why you would like to have the position
● why your employment would benefit the company.

Letters of application are sales letters. You should therefore aim to capture the reader's attention. At the end of the letter, request an interview.

Your letter of application, like all modern business letters, should be designed for easy reading. It should not be overly formal or unnecessarily complicated. Each point should be in a separate paragraph. Keep your letter short and to the point. Remember that the person you write to may be extremely busy and will not want to waste time reading anything irrelevant. The layout for a typical UK letter of application is shown in Figure 1. There are notes explaining it on page 11. How does the layout in Figure 1 differ from the layout for a letter in your country?

Figure 1:
Typical letter of application

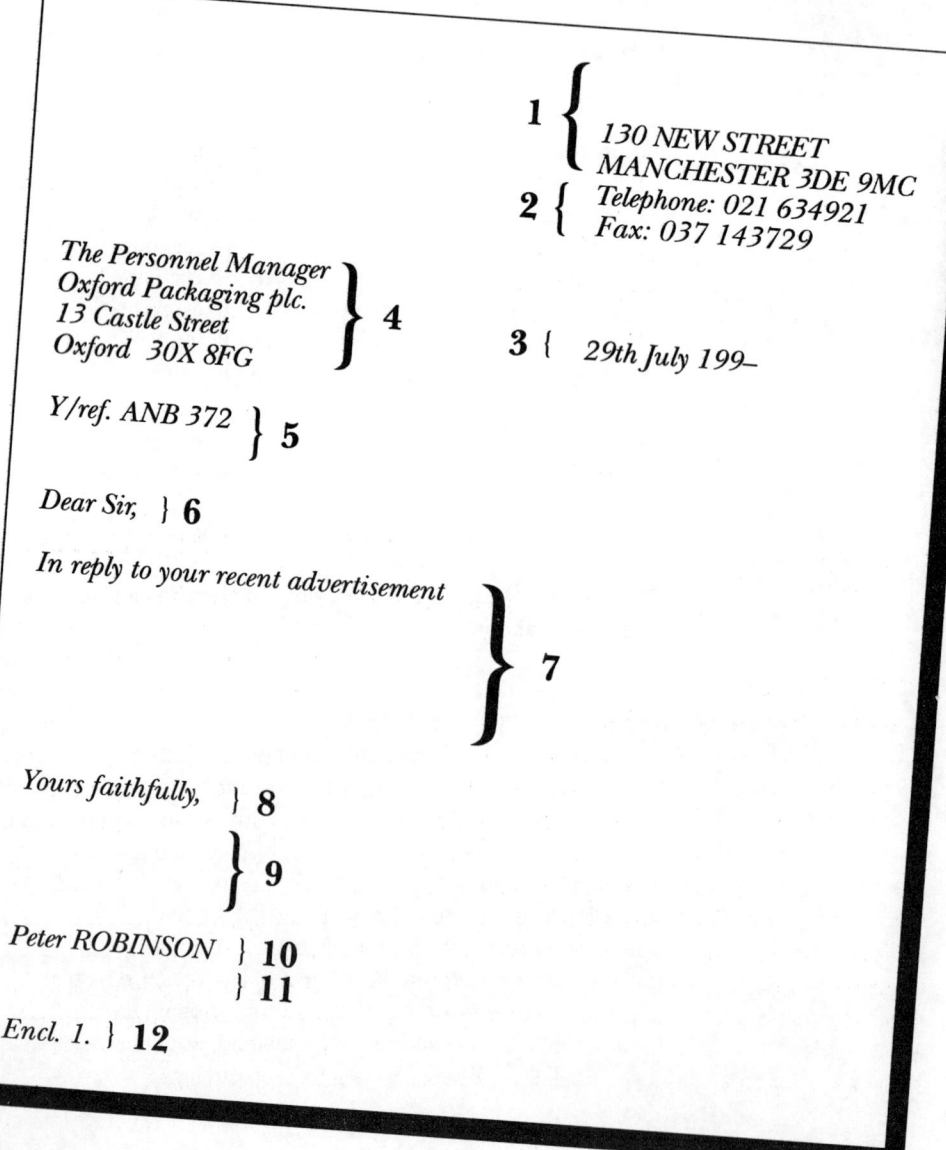

1. THE LETTER HEAD

The address (but not the name) of the person sending the letter. The letter head may be in the top right-hand corner, the top centre or the top left-hand corner.

2. TELEPHONE – TELEX – FAX

Situated immediately below the letter head.

3. THE DATE

If the letter head is situated in the top left-hand corner, the date should be below. Otherwise it should be on the right of the page. In Britain there are three ways to write the date:

- 12th April 1992
- 12 April 1992
- April 12 1992

Americans usually write the month before the day. Avoid using all-number dates as they may be ambiguous. For example 12.4.1992 means 12th April 1992 for a British person but 4th December 1992 for an American.

4. THE INSIDE ADDRESS

This is the address of the person to whom you are writing. It may include the name of the person and/or his or her position and/or the name of the organisation where he or she works. The inside address must be on the left-hand side of the page.

5. REFERENCES

If you are replying to a letter or an advertisement which contains a reference you should include this in your correspondence. This will help your correspondent find the correct file. You may also wish to include your own reference. Both *your reference* and *their reference* should be situated below the inside address.

6. THE OPENING SALUTATION

There are several possibilities. They are as follows:

Dear Sir,	Dear Mr. Baker,
Dear Sirs,	Dear Mrs. Baker,
Sir,	Dear Miss Baker,
Dear Madam,	Dear Ms. Baker,

After the opening salutation, the British write a comma (,) whereas Americans write a colon (:).

7. THE BODY OF THE LETTER

Clear, concise, relevant, easy to read.

8. THE CLOSING SALUTATION

In Britain, if the opening salutation does not mention the name of the correspondent the closing salutation is *Yours faithfully*. If it does mention the name, the closing salutation is *Yours sincerely*. Amercians have several variations such as *Sincerely yours, Respectfully yours* and *Cordially yours*, depending on the circumstances. The closing salutation is situated on the left or in the middle and is followed by a comma.

9. THE SIGNATURE

10. THE AUTHOR'S NAME

Signatures are not always clear. It is therefore essential to write your name below the signature and indicate whether your are a man or woman, for example, Peter Robinson or Mr. P Robinson.

11. YOUR TITLE

Immediately below the name. This is only necessary if you are using company headed paper.

12. ENCLOSURES

If the envelope contains enclosures (a CV, an application form, a diploma, etc), this should be indicated in the bottom left-hand corner of the page. The usual forms are *Enc.* or *Encl.* followed by the number of documents enclosed.

I.3.D
*Discussion
and writing*

The CV/resumé (US): layout

There are no fixed rules for the preparation of a CV, or resumé as it is called in America. Your objective is to present your background and credentials in their most favourable light. Two typical layouts are presented in Figures 2 and 3.

Figure 2:
A typical CV

Pascale VOISIN
7 rue Paul Valéry
22000 SAINT BRIEUC
FRANCE

Tel: (33) 96 47 25 47 (English spoken)

EDUCATION

1990/1992: **Nantes Graduate School of Management**. France
Major French Graduate School of Business and Management.

1988/1990: Preparation HEC in Lyon; special program leading to a competitive examination for entry to a Graduate School of Management.

1988/1989: Baccalaureat C (maths and physics), French equivalent of the Higher Leaving Certificate (A levels).

WORK EXPERIENCE

April, May, June 1992: **IBM France.** Executive Traineeship, Marketing department in Paris: in charge of a marketing study to determine the computer software needs of magazines and other media.

January, February, March 1992: **LACTEL** (second biggest milk producer in France), Marketing study in order to analyse the long-life milk market in Nantes.

October, November, December 1991: **GSI** (company which develops and sells software packages for other companies), Marketing study on the image of GSI's products (software for human resources management) and its position compared to its main competitors.

June, July, August 1991: **Alain MANOUKIAN** (French clothing company). Executive Traineeship. Export department: responsible for the Swiss market: signing of contracts; compiling a sales book explaining what should be used to improve sales performance; drawing up of operating accounts forecasts for new clients.

September 1990: **Charles JOURDAN** (up-market French shoe company). Traineeship. Work with manual workers and entry of clients data on computer. Analysis of the work relationship inside the plant.

July 1989: **BNP** (largest French bank). Traineeship as teller, opening of accounts, dealing with foreign currencies, etc.

LANGUAGES

French: Native language
English: Fluent English: 11 years of practice. Several trips to England.
German: Good knowledge: 9 years of practice.
Spanish: Second year of intensive courses at the Nantes Graduate School of Management.

COMPUTER SKILLS

Symphony, Windows and Word software.

(**Figure 2** continued)

OUTSIDE ACTIVITIES

1990/1992: Responsible for the communication of the Marketing Club of Nantes (Junior Entreprise) which carries out marketing studies for companies.

1990/1991: Organisation of a project developing corporate sponsorship including: a conference; several art exhibitions in local firms (BULL, NANTES INTERNATIONAL AIRPORT, SNCF – French Railways, EDF-GDF – Gas and Electricity utilities and CREDIT LYONNAIS – Bank); Gala dinner.

January to June 1992: Member of IBM Club.

SPORTS

SKIING: 12 years of competition. Competition level.

ATHLETICS: Nationwide school championships.

OTHER INFORMATION

Date of Birth: 22 May 1969

Nationality: French

Figure 3: A typical CV

CURRICULUM VITAE

June RICHMOND
103 Robert Circle
Metuchen,
New Jersey 08840
(908) 549-6133

EDUCATION	Ph.D University of Illinois	1994 (expected date) **French Literature**
	M.A. Montclair State College	1989 **French and Quebec Literatures**
	B.A. Montclair State College	1981 **French Translation, English**

POSITIONS HELD	French Instructor	University of Illinois	1990–1992
	French Instructor	Montclair State College	1988–1989
	Assistant	Foreign Language Lab MSC	1986–1988
	French Translator	Hoffman International Inc., N.J.	1981–1985
	Supervisor	R.H. Bruskin Assoc. N.J.	1979–1981

SPECIAL FIELDS	Nineteenth and Twentieth Century French Literature
	Twentieth Century Quebec Literature
	French Translation and Interpretation

1 In pairs, read the two CVs and discuss with your partner the strengths and weaknesses of each. Which of the two do you prefer? The following criteria may be useful: clarity, layout, information content, conciseness.

2 Write out your own CV.

1.3.E
Writing

Writing a letter of application and CV

Choose one of the recruitment advertisements shown in Figure 4. They all appeared in the *Classified Ads* section of last Saturday's *Daily News*. Apply for the position, writing a CV and cover letter. You may use either real or fictitious information.

The following expressions may help you:

Opening paragraph

- I am writing to you in response to ...
- I wish to apply for the position of ...
- Your advertisement in last Saturday's Daily News ...
- With reference to ...

- Following ...
- Further to ...

Closing paragraph

- I would be happy to have the opportunity ...
- Should you require any further information ...
- I would be most grateful for a chance to ...
- I look forward to hearing from you.

Figure 4:
Recruitment advertisements

JASON WILDE
SALES & MARKETING MANAGER

JASON WILDE, top fashion designer, seeks an international Sales & Marketing Manager. The position requires flair, a working use of foreign languages and a truly international vision to take this prestigious design house further in its developments.

We are seeking a person to promote sales worldwide. Knowledge of the current markets would be preferred. However, we should be happy to meet outstanding applicants with relevant marketing skills in other sectors. Please send resumé and letter (in English only) to:

Yoann CHEVALIER Esq. **JASON WILDE**
86–96 Upper Regents Drive
LONDON SW5 5QS, ENGLAND

GRADUATES, A GREAT CAREER IN AUDITING

Forget the traditional idea of audit. Here, it is a project-based role involving in-depth analysis, assessment and evaluation of our London-based operations. No specific degree discipline is required, just an excellent and consistent academic track record. You will receive one month of intensive training in New York. Upon returning to London you will join a team working on assignments that will expose you to most of the critical areas of our business.

Starting salary £15K plus a profit-sharing bonus after one year's service. Generous mortgage subsidies are also available.

Apply in writing with CV to:
Mr. R. Grey, Northover Merchant Bank, 1 Cheam Road, London EC2 7AG.

Alternatively, you can telephone 071 325 2212 for more information.

(**Figure 4** continued)

PUBLIC RELATIONS
A HIGHER PROFILE/A STRONGER IDENTITY
London £25,000 + lease car

As one of Europe's main transporters with over half a million customers, good public relations are extremely important to our business.

We're now looking for an enthusiastic person to be involved in writing press releases on a variety of subjects, answering newspaper, radio and television enquiries, and assisting with various special projects such as improving internal communication.

With experience gained at a local newspaper or in the public relations department of a large company, you should preferably have a degree in communication or closely related discipline.

Starting salary will be £25,000 which is supported by an excellent range of benefits including profit-sharing and sharesave schemes, 27 days' holiday, lease car, pension, sports and social facilities, and relocation assistance where appropriate.

If you are interested in this opportunity please telephone 081 333 5729 (24-hour answering service), quoting reference 737PQS/G or write to Ms. Janet SIMMS at:

WINGS AND FINS (EUROPE)
142, Pigeon Lane
LONDON, SW1 133

AN EQUAL OPPORTUNITY EMPLOYER

I.3.F

Discussion

A career plan

In groups, discuss your career plans. Explain what you hope to be doing in five/ten/fifteen years' time, and the stages you need to complete in order to achieve your ambitions.

If you have difficulty planning that far ahead, the following headings could serve as a guide:

- sector of activity
- size of company
- geographical location
- expected salary
- department or service

In each case justify your choice.

The following expressions may be useful:

- I hope ...
- I expect ...
- I intend ...
- I plan ...
- I'll need to ...

- After finishing ...
- After I graduate ...
- My short-term goals ...
- I'll have to ...
- I'll try to ...

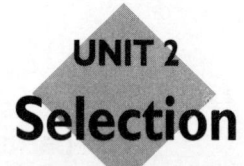

UNIT 2
Selection

The interview

2.1.A
Warm-up

Interviewing and testing

In small groups discuss the following questions:

1 What is the purpose of a job interview?
2 Why is good interviewing important?
3 Could a job interview be replaced by a test?

2.1.B
Reading

Selection

Read the following passage then work on exercises 2.1.C and 2.1.D.

When someone applies for a job they are usually required to send a CV and a cover letter. Some companies also require applicants to fill in an application form. The applicants are then screened and, in some cases, they are asked to take an aptitude test such as a typing test or a sales skills test. Occupational psychology testing is occasionally carried out along with IQ tests and analyses of handwriting.

The next stage in the selection process usually involves an interview. The aim of the interview is to determine whether the prospective employee:

- has the necessary qualifications for the job under consideration.
- has the motivation to meet the company's expectations.
- 'fits' the existing company culture.

A good interviewer attempts to clarify every area of uncertainty, such as any anomalies in the application form, or any points which cannot be checked with a paper and pencil test. The interview is the place where doubts can be aired, questions put and possible misunderstandings rectified.

The interview is also the place where the prospective employee and employer look each other over. Just as the individual is interviewed by the company so the company is also interviewed by the individual. Both parties are therefore on their best behaviour and may not be showing their true colours.

Various interview techniques may be used to find out what an applicant is really like:

- *Job knowledge questions* are asked to find out whether the applicant possesses knowledge essential to the job performance.
- *Job simulation questions* ask the applicant to simulate some aspect of the job performance to see if he or she understands the different facets of the actual task performance.
- *Situational questions* evaluate the applicant's reaction to a specific situation, either job-related or general.

- **Work willingness questions** attempt to determine the applicant's motivation and availability to work.
- **Open-ended questions** encourage the applicant to open up and reveal attitudes and behaviour which may otherwise have remained hidden.
- **Stress interviewing** puts the applicant under pressure by a variety of means. The rationale is twofold: firstly, her or his facade may crack and the 'real' person will appear; and secondly, it may be valuable to see how she or he copes with stress.

Whichever techniques are used it is essential that the interviewer takes the time to prepare his or her interviews. This means acquiring a thorough understanding of the job being offered and making a careful review of all the information contained in the applicant's file (CV, cover letter, application form, references, test results, etc). A thorough and fair interview is an excellent investment.

2.1.C
Discussion

Testing and stress interviewing

1 Several types of test are mentioned in the article in exercise 2.1.B. In groups, discuss any experience you have had of testing as part of a selection procedure:

- describe the test
- what was it measuring?
- was it reliable?

2 In groups, discuss any experience you have had of stress interviewing:

- describe the stress interview
- what was it measuring?
- was it reliable?

2.1.D
Analysis

Interview techniques

Classify the interview questions on this page and page 18 under these headings:

- job knowledge questions
- job simulation questions or situational questions
- work willingness questions
- open-ended questions
- stress interviewing

1 Tell me about the distribution network for luxury sportswear in South East Asia.
2 You have two minutes to convince me I'm crazy.
3 Tell me something about yourself.
4 Sell me your tie.
5 What would you do if one of your salespeople wasn't reaching the sales targets?
6 Make me laugh.
7 What is important to you in a job?
8 What are your main qualities?
9 How much experience have you had using spreadsheets?

10 How would you motivate a team of salespeople?

11 What are your long-range goals?

12 Judging by the way you dress, I'd say you were somebody who never takes risks.

13 How do you feel about working away from home for three months in the year?

14 What is it you don't like about me?

15 How do you handle pressure?

16 How do you feel after a failure?

Think of other questions which could be classified under the above headings.

<table>
<tr><td>2.1.E</td><td rowspan="2"><h1>Body language</h1></td></tr>
<tr><td>Discussion</td></tr>
</table>

2.1.E

Discussion

Body language

Some psychologists have calculated that during a discussion we communicate our feelings and thoughts as follows:

- 7% by means of words
- 38% by means of intonation
- 55% by means of body language

Work in small groups. Place the following behavioural cues in the grid below:

The applicant:

1 taps his foot quickly up and down
2 lights up a cigar
3 searches for his words
4 is trembling
5 has regular eye contact with the interviewer

6 frowns and scratches his head
7 sits back in his chair with his legs outstretched
8 sits with his arms and legs crossed
9 keeps swallowing
10 uses his hands and face to help express himself.

Applicant is nervous	Applicant is unsure
Applicant is confident	Applicant is overconfident

1 Can you find any other behavioural cues which might fit into this grid?

2 Does body language vary form country to country? Try to find examples of how people from different countries express themselves non-verbally.

2.1.F
Role play

Mini interviews

Make a copy of the grid below and use it for the following role play.

Type of question	Frequency	Applicant's reactions			
		nervous	unsure	confident	overconfident
Job knowledge					
Job simulation or situational					
Work-willingness					
Open-ended					
Stress interview					

You are about to take part in a series of mini interviews. In groups of four:

- one student is the interviewer
- one student is the applicant
- two students are observers.

After each interview, the roles rotate.

The interview scenarios are as follows:

- 1st interview: for a sales assistant in a hi-fi store
- 2nd interview: for a trilingual secretary in an import-export department
- 3rd interview: for a PR officer in a large bank
- 4th interview: for a researcher in an R & D department.

The interview role play should last four minutes.

Before the interview
The interviewer and applicant have one minute to prepare the interview.

During the interview
The two observers fill in the grid, noting the frequency of each type of question and the applicant's reactions in each case.

After the interview
After each interview the two observers compare and discuss their observations and should be ready to identify the behavioural cues which influenced them.

Section 2
Other selection criteria

2.2.A
Vocabulary

Attributes

Match the attributes in the left-hand column with their definitions:

Attributes
(S)he is:

1 articulate
2 punctual
3 computer literate
4 tactful
5 scrupulous
6 astute
7 tenacious
8 charismatic
9 outgoing
10 tough
11 numerate
12 outstanding
13 ruthless

(S)he has:
14 drive
15 commitment
16 flair
17 foresight

Definitions

a able to attract, influence and inspire others
b able to anticipate future events
c careful not to offend or upset others
d remarkable and very impressive
e determined and does not give up easily
f naturally able to do something well
g without pity
h fair and honest
i has a strong belief in an idea or system
j can use a range of computer software
k acquainted with the basic principles of mathematics
l expresses herself easily and well
m strong and independent
n motivated and persistent
o clever and skilful
p friendly and open
q arrives on time

In small groups, discuss which of the above attributes you have, you wish to have, or you will need to have in your career.

2.2.B
Analysis 1

Analysing handwriting

Produce a sample of your handwriting for analysis. Spend four minutes copying the text on 'Selection' (page 16). Use a clean sheet of unlined paper. Do not write your name. When the four minutes are over, stop writing and hand in your paper to the teacher.

2.2.C
Listening

Graphology

Listen to the tape recording of a graphologist talking about the basics of graphology. Copy the grid on page 21 on to your own paper and write down as many key words as you can to describe the writer's personality.

Handwriting characteristics		Key words regarding writer's personality
Layout	close to the left wide margin many spaces few spaces	
Size of letters	small letters large letters	
Slope of lines	upward sloping (slight) upward sloping (extreme) downward sloping	
Pressure	heavy pressure light pressure very light pressure	
Slope of letters	upright forward sloping backward sloping very regular	
Joins between letters	smoothly joined badly joined	
Speed	rapid very rapid slow very slow	
Shape of letters	calligraphic simple complicated angular round open rounds	

2.2.D

Analysis 2

Analysing handwriting (continued)

Work in small groups. The teacher will randomly distribute one handwriting sample to each group. Analyse the handwriting and decide whether the writer would be suitable or unsuitable for a position in your company.

Listening

Methods of recruitment and selection

Listen to the tape recording of recruiters describing how their organisations recruit and select personnel. Copy the grid below on to your own paper and fill it in as you listen.

	1st recruiter	2nd recruiter	3rd recruiter
1 recruiter's position			
2 organisation			
3 position(s) discussed			
4 recruiting sources			
5 typical response level			
6 screening criteria			
7 people encountered during 1st interview			
8 people encountered during 2nd interview			
9 tests			
10 other criteria mentioned			

2.2.F
Vocabulary

Money and people

Divide the following terms into money-linked and people-linked terms then match each with its definition.

Terms

1 Personnel Manager

2 commission

3 wage

4 senior executive

5 retainer

6 middle manager

7 fee

8 salary

9 bonus

10 deputy

11 Human Resource Manager

12 fringe benefits

13 profit sharing

14 pro rata

15 supervisor

16 piecework

17 raise

18 Dean

Definitions

a A system whereby employees receive a proportion of the company's profits.

b Somebody whose power and responsibility are used chiefly to implement the broad goals set by top management.

c Payment for services based upon number of hours worked or number of units produced.

d Somebody engaged in acquiring personnel, preparing them for work, overseeing their performance, and providing compensation.

e A second-in-command.

f Compensation for part-time work expressed as a percentage of full-time pay.

g A charge or payment for a service or privilege

h Somebody whose responsibility for personnel includes strategic planning.

i Somebody who oversees another's work.

j Compensation based on the number of units produced.

k A compensation payment in addition to regular wages or salary.

l A fixed sum paid to an agent regardless of performance.

m Compensation based upon time worked for a week, month or year rather than for an hour.

n Benefits other than wages, salaries and bonuses, often known as 'perks'.

o Compensation based on an agent's sales performance.

p Somebody who has the most supervisory authority and responsibility in an organisation.

q An increase in wage or salary.

r The head of a university faculty.

2.2.G
Case study

The right person for the job

Look at these pages from Jardina's company report and its catalogue. They give details of the company's retail outlets and product lines.

Jardina is a Paris-based manufacturer of garden equipment. Founded in the early 1980s by a young engineer, Jacques Bernard, the company has flourished, doubling its turnover every five years. Jacques Bernard is now Managing Director. Sales last year reached 10 million French francs, the equivalent of £1 million. The company averages two new product launches per year.

The main retail outlets for Jardina's products are:

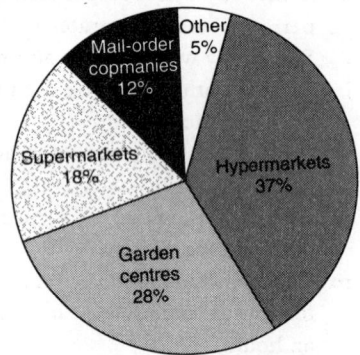

The remaining 5% of the firm's production is bought by a Kuwaiti importer for distribution in the Middle East.

SPRING CATALOGUE 1992

CONTENTS

On a recent trip to Britain, Jacques Bernard discovered that while small garden items such as window boxes and hanging baskets were similar to those found on the French market, garden furniture in Britain tended to be old-fashioned, over-priced and of inferior quality compared to Jardina's products. On his return to Paris he asked his Marketing Director, Pierre André, to carry out an extensive market study to see whether is would be feasible for Jardina to enter the British market, and if so, what would be the best approach to take.

By early December the study was finished and placed on Jacques Bernard's desk. The British market looked promising. Over the next two weeks the marketing strategy was developed, checked and fine-tuned and on Christmas Eve the two men drank a toast to Queen Elizabeth.

In the New Year Jardina's Personnel Officer contacted Austin Livingstone Selection in London. Two weeks later the following advertisement appeared in a well-known national newspaper.

Figure 5:
Advertisement for Jardina

Sales Manager

Jardina

Already one of the fastest-growing garden products companies in France, Jardina will soon be selling its latest range of high-quality garden furniture in Britain.

We are looking for an experienced Sales Manager to set up a distributorship in Great Britain. This will involve developing a national sales force (8 representatives initially) and planning marketing concepts in conjunction with the Marketing Director.

To be successful you must have good sales and communication skills, be able to manage people effectively and have an excellent track record. A working knowledge of French would be an advantage.

Salary will be within the range £16K–£18K plus an excellent incentive scheme and fringe benefits in keeping with the image of a young, dynamic company.

Interested? For an informal discussion contact our advising consultant Mark Livingstone on 071 342 2832. Alternatively, write to:

Austin Livingstone Selection,
15th Floor,
Manor Heights,
Manor Road,
London,
N3ED 4AX.

By the end of February Austin Livingstone had received 150 applications, interviewed 23 people and shortlisted four of them. They then sent the following details of each of the shortlisted applicants to Jardina in Paris. In spite of his mediocre English Jacques Bernard intends to interview each of the four applicants.

Figure 6:
Applicants for job at Jardina

AUSTIN LIVINGSTONE SELECTION

CLIENT: JARDINA

POSITION: SALES MANAGER

NAME:	Derek HAMPER
NATIONALITY:	British
AGE:	30
DOMICILE:	Swansea, South Wales
MARITAL STATUS:	Married; 3 children
QUALIFICATIONS:	A levels in maths, physics and chemistry; B.Sc. in Chemical Engineering; M.Sc. in Marketing
PROFESSIONAL EXPERIENCE:	3 m traineeship as a sales assistant in a Bournemouth department store 4 y Research assistant for a large chemical group 3 y Product development officer for the same company 2 m traineeship in a Market Research agency
LANGUAGES:	English; some notions of French
INTERESTS:	Rugby (plays regularly with local team); member of the church board of directors with special responsibilities for fund-raising.
FURTHER INFORMATION:	Imaginative, energetic and ambitious. Very outward-going. Works especially well in a team. A tall (1m95), well-built man whose very presence commands respect. Seems set on a marketing career.

AUSTIN LIVINGSTONE SELECTION

CLIENT: JARDINA

POSITION: SALES MANAGER

NAME:	Anne GUENO
DOMICILE:	London
NATIONALITY:	French
MARITAL STATUS:	Single
AGE:	26
QUALIFICATIONS:	Baccalauréat C (High school final exam specialising in maths and science) Ecole Supérieure de Commerce (Graduate Business School) diploma
PROFESSIONAL EXPERIENCE:	2 m traineeship in a supermarket as a cashier 2 m traineeship as a sales assistant in a garden centre in London 1 y member of a regional sales team for a cosmetic company 3 y P.A. to the Marketing Director of a London-based manufacturer of fitted kitchens and bathrooms.
LANGUAGES:	French, English, German
INTERESTS:	Cinema, music (plays the clarinet), skiing (has won several amateur competitions), hang-gliding.
FURTHER INFORMATION:	Extremely dynamic and confident. Lives in a penthouse in a very fashionable district of London. Drives a Ferrari. Dresses flamboyantly. Brother is a senior executive for a furniture chain in Britain, sister is chief purchasing officer for a leisure goods retail group.

AUSTIN LIVINGSTONE SELECTION

CLIENT: JARDINA

POSITION: SALES MANAGER

NAME: John HOLMES

DOMICILE: Reading

NATIONALITY: British

MARITAL STATUS: Divorced. Children grown up

AGE: 52

QUALIFICATIONS: None

PROFESSIONAL EXPERIENCE:
14 y sales representative for a German toy manufacturer
6 y chief buyer for the toy department of a famous London store
6 y regional Sales Manager for a double-glazing firm
9 y Sales Director for the U.K. division of an American food giant.

LANGUAGES: English, some German.

INTERESTS: Archaeology, trekking in the mountains, reading, classical music, cooking.

FURTHER INFORMATION:
Left school at 15 following death of parents.
A self-taught intellectual with an extensive cultural repertoire.
Rather reserved; speaks quietly and dresses soberly.
Lives alone in a small flat in the centre of Reading.
Loves France and the French.
Would like to retire in the Pyrenees.

AUSTIN LIVINGSTONE SELECTION

POSITION: SALES MANAGER

CLIENT: JARDINA

NATIONALITY: British

NAME: Ruth BENNET

AGE: 36

DOMICILE: San Francisco

MARITAL STATUS: Married; 2 children

QUALIFICATIONS:
A levels (Art, French, English literature)
B.A. in interior design
Currently completing an MBA (majoring in marketing)

PROFESSIONAL EXPERIENCE:
2 y Interior Designer for a small design centre in a London suburb.
8 y Ran her own furniture showroom and design centre in a S.F. suburb.

LANGUAGES: English, French (rather rusty)

INTERESTS: Horseriding, tennis, being with her children.

FURTHER INFORMATION:
A very strong entrepreneurial spirit.
Set up her own SF-based business which was rather successful until her partner began using the premises for dealing cocaine.
Wants to return to Britain after 10 years in the States.

When you have read all the information about Jardina, carry out the following role play and discussion.

1 In groups of five, perform a role play in which one of you is Jacques Bernard and the other four are the applicants detailed in the client record cards shown on **pages 26 and 27**.

2 If you are Jacques Bernard, study the information on the shortlisted applicants and prepare your interviews. What further information do you need about each applicant? Are there any uncertainties you wish to clear up before making an appointment? Prepare your interview questions accordingly.

3 Interview each of the applicants. (You have a maximum of eight minutes per applicant, so manage your time effectively.)

4 After the four applicants have been interviewed, discuss the following questions in your groups:

   ● What are the pros and cons of each applicant?
   ● Which of the four do you think would be most suitable for this key position? Why?

5 Compare your findings with the other groups.

2.2.H
Writing

A letter of rejection

Write a letter of rejection to one of the applicants, explaining as tactfully as possible why his or her application was unsuccessful.

The following expressions may be useful:

● We are sorry to inform you ...
● I am afraid that we shall be unable ...
● It is with the utmost regret ...
● Your application ... has been unsuccessful
● a difficult decision ...
● an exacting task ...
● other highly-qualified candidates ...
● We would like to thank you ...

Motivating personnel

Section 1

Motivation

Factors which motivate me

1 The following questionnaire was given to staff at different levels in a number of US companies. Fill it in by placing a ✓ next to the six items which motivate you most in your work. Compare your response with another person's list.

1		Job security
2		Respect for me
3		Adequate rest periods
4		Good pay
5		Pleasant working conditions
6		Chance to turn out quality work
7		Good atmosphere
8		Having a local employee paper
9		Chance for promotion
10		Having interesting work
11		Pensions, health care, etc
12		Not having to work too hard
13		Good internal communication
14		Feeling my job is important
15		Having an employee council
16		Having a written job description
17		Being praised by my boss
18		Being assessed
19		Being involved in decision-making
20		Agreement with organization's objectives
21		Opportunity for self-development
22		Generous vacation arrangements
23		Sanctions for poor performance
24		Having a supportive supervisor
25		Having a lot of freedom

2 Can you think of any other factors which motivate? Rank your three most important items.

3.1.B
Analysis

Motivation

Study Table 2 which shows the results of the questionnaire in exercise 3.1.A for three different occupational groups: managers, senior level executives and secretaries.

1 What interesting facts emerge?

2 How do these results differ from your personal results? Your group's results?

3 How could a Personnel Manager or Human Resources Manager use this information?

Table 2:

Survey results for managers, senior level executives and secretaries

	Managers A	Senior level executives B	Secretaries C	
1				Job security
2	✓	✓	✓	Respect for me
3				Adequate rest periods
4	✓	✓		Good pay
5				Pleasant working conditions
6	✓			Chance to turn out quality work
7				Good atmosphere
8				Having a local employee paper
9				Chance for promotion
10		✓	✓	Having interesting work
11				Pension, health care, etc
12				Not having to work too hard
13				Good internal communication
14	✓	✓	✓	Feeling my job is important
15				Having an employee council
16				Having a written job description
17			✓	Being praised by my boss
18				Being assessed
19				Being involved in decision-making
20				Agreement with organization's objectives
21	✓	✓	✓	Opportunity for self-development
22				Generous vacation arrangements
23				Sanctions for poor performance
24				Having a supportive supervisor
25	✓	✓	✓	Having a lot of freedom

Vocabulary

Work conditions

Fill in each blank with one of the terms from the following list:

deadlines	fulfilment	redundancies
turnover	output	boredom
subsidised	membership	subcontractor
shift	standard of living	pension

This industry is characterised by high trade union _____1_____
and low staff _____2_____ in a region where the
_____3_____ is below the national average. Our
company is a leading _____4_____ to the big automobile
firms, which means that delivery _____5_____ are
becoming tighter and the threat of _____6_____ greater.
This puts a great deal of pressure on workers. They work on a
_____7_____ system, which maximises the plant's
_____8_____ but which is very tiring as the shifts are
particularly long. We have a _____9_____ canteen and a
generous _____10_____ scheme but workers complain of
_____11_____ and a lack of _____12_____
in their work.

Listening

Motivating employees

1 Listen to the tape recording in which managers describe how their company
motivates its employees. Copy the grid on page 32 on to your own paper
and fill it in as you listen.

2 Listen to the three managers again and answer the following questions:

1st manager

1 Why do you think the letters were hand delivered to the worker's wives?

2 Why were the workers put into groups?

3 Do you think the campaign was an appropriate way to solve Goodyear's
personnel problems? Could it work in other companies?

2nd manager

1 The first part of the Dean's campaign was not very popular and many
professors criticised it. What arguments do you think they presented to
persuade him to modify his new policy?

2 What do you see as the main advantages and disadvantages of the second
part of the campaign, from the point of view of both the school and the
professors?

3rd Manager

1 Why is a leaving interview an interesting source of information for the company? What kind of information would you expect a leaving interview to reveal?

2 Can you think of any other ways that the company could have developed an atmosphere of mutual trust?

	1st Manager	2nd Manager	3rd Manager
Organisation			
Category of employees concerned			
Problem			
Cause(s) of problem			
Strategies employed			
Results			

Role play

Managing human resources at Zephyr

You are a management consultant and have just been given the following information about a company called Zephyr. Read the information and then carry
out the role play which follows.

Zephyr is a medium-sized company based in the South-East of England, a region of
high growth and relatively low unemployment. Most of its 372 production line workers are involved in the assembly of high-quality electronic components for the automobile industry for which Zephyr has been a subcontractor since before the Second
World War. The workers as a whole enjoy similar pay and status to other semi-skilled
workers in the area. Sixty per cent of the workers belong to a trade union, and union
membership has increased significantly during the past six months.

The plant operates on a shift system, a typical week being composed of five eight-
hour shifts with one 10-minute tea break and one 30-minute lunch break per shift.
The factory is modern, with air conditioning, controlled humidity, diffused lighting
and soberly painted grey walls. The workshops are spacious, each worker having his
own bench and tools for the assembly operations. There are two canteens, one for the
workers and one for the management, with subsidised meals and drinks in both.

New recruits are given a three-day training course during which they learn the
basic operations of assembly work. They develop speed and dexterity with practice.
Apart from this there is no systematic training given to workers. Shop-floor supervisors indicate that Pakistani and Indian immigrants quickly develop speed. Language
barriers, though, prevent them from integrating fully into the culture of the firm.
Other workers often complain that the immigrants work too hard.

Almost three-quarters of the plant's workers are between 18 and 24 years of age,
and of these 69% are women. The basic rate of pay depends on length of service in the
company; workers receive annual increments of 10%. The average length of service is
seven years and the annual staff turnover is 20% although this is increasing all the
time. Delivery delays have occasionally occurred as a result.

Incentive bonuses are paid to each worker according to the number of components
he or she assembles above a certain monthly quota, and they are expressed as a percentage of his or her basic salary. A highly productive worker may earn an extra 10%
of his wage in bonus payments, but most workers typically earn between 3% and 5%,
with some earning no bonus at all because of failure to reach the quota.

Zephyr's sales have been in steady decline since the mid 1960s when the British
automobile industry began to disintegrate. Equally worrying is the decline in output
per worker, despite Zephyr's heavy investment in new technology. Several attempts
have been made to diversify, especially in the area of components for domestic appliances (washing machines, hair dryers, etc) but with limited success. Three years ago
the company was forced to dismiss 150 workers; this was done on a last-in-first-out
(LIFO) basis, and now it is feared that more redundancies are imminent. One of the
most common subjects discussed in the canteen is whether or not the plant will close
down. Rumours of workers experiencing nervous breakdowns have been circulating;
the number of workers on sick leave has actually increased.

The Managing Director of Zephyr, Mr John Hurd, is hoping to avoid further
redundancies and has been negotiating with top officials of a Nissan plant which is
due to open in South Wales in 18 months' time. It appears that Zephyr's chances of
doing business with Nissan are good, its reputation for quality components being
highly appreciated by the Japanese car giant.

In negotiating with the Japanese Mr Hurd has discussed changes in human
resources management. In concrete terms this means that Zephyr will have to become
more competitive by raising productivity by 10% while maintaining high-quality standards and respecting very tight delivery deadlines – a seemingly impossible task in
view of its recent poor productivity record.

Now carry out the following role play.

1 Imagine you are a management consultant who has to meet Mr Hurd to advise him on the best course of action to take.

   a Before your meeting with Mr Hurd, write a list of questions you wish to ask him in order to help you analyse the problems(s) in greater depth. When you have finished your list, read your questions aloud to the class.

   Example

> Who leaves the company and why? Why is there no ongoing training?

   b Describe what you see as Zephyr's problem(s) and explain the possible causes.

   Example

> There is a high staff turnover which is bad for morale and may be due to a lack of promotion prospects.

   c In small groups, outline a plan to improve Zephyr's situation.

2 Choose one member from each group to play the role of Mr Hurd. He or she has a maximum of five minutes to make a presentation to the Zephyr employees. He or she should:

   ● present the plan he or she hopes to implement, justifying it where necessary
   ● be prepared to answer any questions the employees may have.

3 Imagine you are Production Manager for Nissan. Decide which of the presentations was the most convincing. Justify your decision.

Section 2

Working overseas

3.2.A

Warm-up

Overseas assignments

Before you read the passage in exercise 3.2.B, discuss these questions in groups:

1 Have you ever lived or worked overseas? Was it a short-term or long-term stay? Did you experience any difficulties adjusting to the different culture?

2 Do you have any plans for working abroad? What advantages do you see in working abroad? What might be the particular difficulties you encounter? Do you feel well enough prepared for an overseas assignment?

3 How can companies help their personnel prepare for an overseas assignment?

4 From what you know about Americans, would you say they find it easier or more difficult than people from your country to adjust to a foreign culture? Why are some expatriates more at ease than others?

Training global managers

Read the article below and find the answers to the questions which follow.

One of the reasons why the Japanese have been so successful in penetrating world markets is that they have understood and responded to the challenges of doing business in alien countries and cultures. Japanese expatriate personnel are far better equipped than their American counterparts for living and working abroad.

In a recent survey, three-quarters of the 80 US corporations responding reported that between 10% and 40% of their personnel assigned overseas had to be recalled or dismissed due to poor performance. Only 14% of the 35 Japanese companies responding reported a failure rate of over 10% and in no case did it reach 20%.

Maintaining a US family overseas costs an average of $200,000 per year. Recalling key personnel is not only expensive but also highly disruptive, often leading to confusion and lost opportunities. Furthermore, an expatriate who is recalled will, in most cases, leave the company even though his or her performance may have been good prior to the overseas assignment. Replacing him or her means that the company has permanently lost a valuable human asset.

Even those US expatriates who complete their assignments may not be working to full capacity and although technically they have not failed, they may be costing their company a great deal in foregone profits.

The reason why Japanese and American expatriates perform so differently may be explained by the better preparation and support which Japanese managers and technicians receive. In Japanese companies, a thorough selection is made at least one year before the assignment is to begin, so that anybody at risk is rejected.

The selection procedure is followed by a training programme where assignees learn the culture, customs, language and ways of doing business in the host country. They learn that they will have to do without many home-country comforts, and to accept, respect and even enjoy inconvenient customs and procedures.

Upon arrival in the country, the Japanese expatriate is assigned a mentor. This is usually a local person who will help the newcomer to settle in and get through the first year or so.

During their assignments Japanese managers or technicians are in constant contact with head office. They are kept up-to-date on any changes that take place during their absence and this reduces any worries about returning home. They also know that their foreign assignments are an integral step in their career plans.

Two-thirds of American companies have no formal training programmes to prepare personnel for overseas work. The other third limit their training to an informational briefing just before departure, but with no simulation activities or question-and-answer sessions with host nationals. Furthermore, no attempt is made to involve the family in preparing themselves for their new environment. Many expatriate personnel are recalled because their spouse or children cannot adapt, and this creates immense pressure on the whole family.

One of the reasons why American companies are so reluctant to set up effective training and support programmes is that a trend has developed to replace expatriate personnel by host-country nationals. However, the increasing globalisation of business has led to a net increase in the number of Americans working overseas, in spite of the trend to replace them. This increase is likely to continue if American headquarters want to maintain and strengthen links with their overseas businesses.

Expatriate personnel may be divided into three categories, each with its own set of needs. Firstly, there are the short-stay technicians engaged in technical assistance or the transfer of technology. Because they rarely stay for more than a few months abroad their needs are mainly limited to techniques for survival. For example, they will need to know something of the uniqueness of the host-country culture and learn to engage in activities which make life in an alien land tolerable.

Secondly, there are the long-term expatriates

whose needs go beyond pure survival. Learning to be effective is a major challenge, and this means knowing what to expect, how to read cues, and how to adjust one's management style to the foreign culture. Furthermore, learning to enjoy the foreign culture is essential in order to avoid culture fatigue.

The third type of expatriate is the foreign national coming to America, and they too have their own needs which must be met.

Any training programme must take into account the different needs of these three groups. It should also be specific to the country of assignment or, in the case of foreign nationals coming to America, the country of origin. Cultural differences encountered in France are very different from those in Russia, Nigeria or Saudi Arabia, and it is the instructor's job to identify these differences, explain why they might be problematic and teach the skills necessary to cope with them and, ultimately, to appreciate them.

1 How do US and Japanese expatriate personnel cope with overseas assignments?

2 What are the costs of the high rate of failure among US expatriates?

3 What do the Japanese do to minimise their failure rate?

4 What training activities are available for American managers and technicians working overseas?

5 What are the three kinds of expatriates and what are their needs?

3.2.C
Discussion

Identifying training needs

I In small groups choose a host country and an expatriate group. Make a list of all the cultural differences which an expatriate and his or her family may encounter in that country and which may be problematic.

Example

Host country:	USA
Expatriate group:	Algerian technicians on a six-month technology transfer assignment
Cultural differences:	food (need to adapt to a diet of highly processed food; difficulties in obtaining basic items)
	sex roles (women have equal status and identical rights)
	smoking (forbidden in public places; frowned upon by many Americans)
	punctuality (for both professional and social activities)
	informality (in dress, use of christian names)

Here are some further ideas to help you get going:

Greetings: How do people greet each other? Do they embrace, shake hands, avoid physical contact? Do they use first names or surnames? Is there a high regard for rank or social position? How is this manifested? Is there a rigid code for greetings or are many things permissible?

Visiting:	If you are invited to somebody's house, are you expected to bring a gift? If so, what? Should you dress formally? Should you offer to clear the table/wash up? Should you return the hospitality/send a note of thanks?
Eating:	Is it rude to decline certain food or drink? Should women accept alcohol? May you eat with your fingers? May you ask for 'seconds'? Is it acceptable to eat with your elbows resting on the table? Should you leave directly after the meal?
Tipping:	Should you tip taxi drivers, porters, doormen, barbers, government employees, bus drivers, petrol(gas) station attendants, others? How much?
Conversing:	Are there any subjects which are taboo? What is considered more important, diplomacy or frankness? How important is it to have a sense of humour? How acceptable is it to tell 'rude' jokes or jokes about racial minorities? Is it considered impolite to discuss somebody's age, weight or personal habits?
Gestures and non-verbal communication:	How close should you stand when conversing? How acceptable is it to touch? How important is eye contact? Are there any gestures you should avoid using?
Dress:	Is it OK to wear shorts to work, sleeveless dresses in the street, hats in-doors, nothing on the beach?
Dates:	Who asks for the date, the man or the woman? Who pays? Is kissing in public acceptable? How significant is a date for a future relationship?

2 Now carry out the following role play.

Imagine you are taking part in a weekend training session to prepare personnel for a forthcoming overseas assignment. Each member of the group in turn will play the role of instructor while the other members of the group play the role of assignees. The instructor must:

- choose one of the cultural differences which the group has listed
- explain why it may be problematic and how best to deal with it
- answer any questions the assignees may have.

3.2.D

Writing

A business report

You have recently been appointed as Personnel and Training Manager of an American multinational corporation. Looking through the files you notice that a large number of your expatriate personnel were recalled from their overseas assignment earlier than planned, and of those who completed their assignment many felt that they would have done a better job if they had been better prepared.

Write a report to your CEO. The objectives of your report are as follows:

- to *describe* the problem
- to *explain* the gravity of the problem
- to *outline* a plan for dealing with it
- to *convince* your CEO that your plan should be adopted.

The report should not exceed two pages and, if possible should be typewritten, double spaced, with 2.5cm margins.

In writing your report, you should respect the following guidelines:

1 Give your report a title. The title should be concise (a maximum of seven words), easy to understand, attractive (include an active verb if possible), and should convey to the reader something about the nature and conclusions of your report. For example, which of the following titles do you think is most effective?

> A study of the recent impact of computers on office workers today
> A bite of the Apple
> Computers are revolutionising office work

2 In the first paragraph, state the reason for your report and the nature of the specific problem to be solved. For example:

> The growing number of AIDS victims has led to an increase in demand among young people for condoms. Corex, Spain, is creating a new product to meet this demand: *Safe and Chic Condoms*. This report presents the company's training requirements in the short and medium terms.

3 Provide the relevant information in convenient form. Make full use of headings and itemised lists in order to call attention to important points and allow the reader to grasp related points easily. For example:

> *Our main training needs are in the following areas:*
> * *the use of new machines*
> * *the new methods of working*
> * *quality circles*
> * *German*

4 Be accurate, specific, dependable, unbiased, well-organised, unambiguous, clear, concise and interesting.

5 In the last paragraph, state the answers to the problems outlined in the first paragraph.

3.2.E

Analysis

Where should you work?

Table 3 refers to the 1991 pay of four different ranks of executives in 20 different countries. They range upwards from junior and middle management in a sizeable division of a big group, to the head of a function such as marketing and finally to the head of the division as a whole.

In each case, the table gives two sets of figures. The first is typical gross pay consisting of salaries plus bonuses which are fixed as opposed to those which vary with profits and so on. The second figure translates the gross pay into buying power.

Buying power is calculated by turning the gross sum into net pay. This is done by deducting tax and similar charges standard for someone of the country who is married with two dependent children, and adding back the normal family allowances. The net pay is then turned into buying power by adjusting for price variances shown by surveys of executives' living costs. The other currencies have been converted to sterling at the rates of 30 September 1991. The different buying power experienced by the different ranks of executives may be seen as a gauge of the incentive in each country to get to the top.

Table 3:
Average rates of pay worldwide

Country	Junior manager		Middle manager		Head of function		Head of division	
	Gross pay £	Buying power £	Gross pay £	Buying power £	Gross pay £	Buying power £	Gross pay £	Buying power £
Hong Kong	18,682	18,267	29,480	27,536	42,635	39,824	63,610	59,415
United States	25,779	23,048	35,326	29,672	48,888	39,165	68,978	52,736
Switzerland	35,385	22,805	46,885	28,722	65,219	37,420	90,079	48,735
Germany (West)	28,497	18,800	39,091	25,774	55,463	35,594	82,339	49,176
Canada	22,823	18,806	31,255	24,074	45,095	32,186	60,014	40,570
France	22,084	16,931	30,829	22,773	44,037	30,579	61,846	41,157
Spain	21,938	15,750	31,186	21,466	44,577	28,668	64,659	37,483
Italy	23,216	14,898	32,681	20,115	47,026	27,275	67,708	37,510
United Kingdom	18,758	15,015	25,017	19,603	35,027	26,163	48,280	34,115
Belgium	24,933	16,141	34,983	20,139	49,900	25,532	71,216	32,624
Netherlands	21,775	15,992	30,274	20,302	42,875	25,553	57,775	31,761
Australia	18,545	15,118	25,455	18,928	33,383	22,746	45,980	29,608
South Africa	12,335	12,966	16,366	16,238	22,804	21,336	31,511	28,229
Ireland	18,993	13,275	25,545	16,323	34,182	20,235	45,315	25,229
New Zealand	13,524	10,827	17,988	14,078	24,059	18,498	32,312	24,509
Finland	22,970	12,156	30,202	14,608	40,480	18,041	53,975	21,998
Denmark	25,289	12,149	32,143	13,888	43,302	16,538	64,799	21,641
Greece	11,657	9,678	16,272	12,794	23,906	18,144	32,294	23,546
Norway	18,954	11,669	25,122	14,055	33,627	16,987	43,496	20,390
Sweden	20,151	10,544	27,560	13,294	37,566	17,009	49,695	21,511

Adapted from *The Financial Times*, 22 November 1991

In small groups, discuss the information which emerges from this table. Which countries do you think use money as an incentive to get to the top?

COMPANY FOCUS
People in BP

Read the following extracts from BP's 1991 Annual Report and answer the questions which follow.

WORLDWIDE

During 1991, we have continued to make changing our culture a priority. BP's employees all over the world are taking part in a process which aims to remove barriers, improve performance and devolve authority. We believe the changes will strengthen our relationship with all the stakeholders in BP: our shareholders, our employees, our customers, our suppliers and the communities in which we operate.

A key element in the change process is the building up of effective communications with our employees. In Europe, we have been successful in integrating teams drawn from up to 14 nationalities. We have also worked effectively across national boundaries in S.E. Asia, where we have established an Asia Pacific regional office in Singapore.

Michelle Martin, warehouse technician, at BP's Prudhoe Bay oilfield in Alaska.

EMPLOYEE INVOLVEMENT

A continuing programme of opinion research among our employees has shown they are keen to become more involved in BP's affairs and to contribute views through two-way communication. Their other concerns are to find ways to enhance job satisfaction and to improve career development prospects in BP's new, flatter organisation. To respond to these aspirations, we are introducing Personal Development Plans to all parts of BP.

EQUAL OPPORTUNITY

It has been BP's policy that all its employees should have equal opportunities for career advancement. In addition to the programmes for our own employees, our work with education gives considerable support for women and those from disadvantaged groups to prepare themselves for careers, particularly in science and engineering.

BP Exploration has launched worldwide its Women's Initiative, which promotes career development by making the working environment more suitable for women and helps them achieve their full potential.

BP Oil is one of the first companies to have joined Opportunity 2000, a campaign to improve the ratio of women to men in the UK workforce. The Springboard Women's Development Programme, started by BP Oil and now used in the group's London offices, is encouraging career development for women in non-managerial grades.

Where practicable, we try to meet the growing demand from employees to provide day-care facilities for their children. In the

Lászlo Németh and Csaba Györfi work at one of BP's new service stations in Budapest, Hungary.

UK, nurseries were opened at several of our major offices outside London and we plan to extend these facilities to other sites in 1992.

In the USA, as part of our 'family friendly' policies (which also support flexitime working), we have taken over the operation of a child-care centre in Alaska. In Cleveland, Ohio, we have arranged to provide replacement care for employees' children when the regular child minders are not available.

In South Africa, we remain fully committed to advancing the careers of our black staff. In the UK, we are the largest sponsor of ethnic minority students by providing work experience through the Windsor Fellowship.

SHARE SCHEMES

In the UK, eligible employees were again invited, in May to participate in the BP share schemes. At the end of 1991, 26,100 current and ex-employees held shares under the schemes. The number of participants rose by 3,000 on the previous year. We launched similar schemes in Australia, New Zealand, Norway, France, Spain and Hong Kong and are encouraged by the high level of response from our employees.

EMPLOYEE INVOLVEMENT

A Long Term Performance Plan was established at the beginning of the year for our senior international executives, including the managing directors, with the aim of linking a significant part of their future remuneration to the creation of long-term value for shareholders.

The annual remuneration of these executives is set in US dollars. However, as they may elect to be paid in the currency of the countries where they work, the remuneration of executives reported in sterling will reflect exchange rate variations from year to year.

Robert Latefa at the wheel during a safety competition for BP drivers at Harare in Zimbabwe.

Rengasamy Velu checking LPG cylinders at the domestic gas bottling plant in Singapore.

IN THE UK
PENSIONS

The BP pension scheme continues to be regarded as a premier scheme. Following a review, we have improved the contributory option, so enabling members to qualify for enhanced benefits. Also, when an employee can no longer work through injury or illness, we have improved the incapacity benefit payable to the employee and his or her dependants.

DISABLED PEOPLE

It is our policy that suitably qualified people with a disability should be able to seek and remain in employment with BP. At the end of 1991, we employed 102 people in the UK who were officially registered as disabled, but there were many more who chose not to register.

BP's performance in health, safety and environmental (HSE) care continues, rightly, to be of close interest to the public, to governments and to our shareholders. We believe our record is a good one. But more and more is being demanded of companies today and we recognise we cannot simply rest on our past reputation. We are therefore striving to make BP an industry leader in HSE performance.

This makes sense not just from a moral standpoint but also as a matter of sound business practice. Today, a good HSE performance is an integral part of efficient and profitable business management. However, for a global company like BP, the aim of being an industry leader in HSE is far from straightforward, because of the differing standards and expectations from country to country. Yet this can also provide an opportunity to secure a competitive edge – for example, by transferring technologies from regions with strict environmental standards to those whose standards are currently less stringent.

In order to recognise and promote outstanding HSE performance by our employees, an annual Chairman's HSE Award has been introduced. Employees worldwide are encouraged to submit HSE projects or initiatives that have given something 'extra' to help progress our vision of better employee health, greater safety to people and property, and a cleaner environment. We believe that efforts such as this will help raise awareness in BP of the critical effect that good HSE performance has on the future of the company.

1 What does a 'flatter organisation' mean (line 26)? What does it imply in terms of hierarchical relationships, individual responsibility and career development?

2 What is Opportunity 2000?

3 What is BP's policy regarding:

- employees' children?
- employees becoming shareholders?
- disabled employees?
- HSE?

What do you think the company gains from these policies?

4 How does BP's policy towards its employees differ from that of companies in which you have worked? Do you think you would enjoy working for a company like BP

PART 11
Marketing

UNIT 4
The Marketing Mix

The four Ps

A recent purchase

In pairs, discuss with your partner a recent purchase you made. What was the product, where did you buy it, how much did it cost and what influenced you in your choice of what to buy and where to buy it?

The Marketing Mix

Read the following passage then work on exercise 4.1.C.

The marketing mix is a blend of four components: product, price, promotion and place. By manipulating these components (often referred to as the four Ps) a marketer can best respond to the needs of customers and thus maximise sales.

Product

Determining consumers' needs and wants and then translating them into desirable products is a marketer's first task. There are many ways to classify products, the most basic distinction being between goods and services. Another distinction is between consumer and industrial items, the markets and purchasing patterns being very different in each case. Consumer products are divided into three subgroups with different marketing tools needed for each:

- Convenience goods and services are products which are readily available, low priced and heavily advertised, and which are purchased quickly and often.
- Shopping goods and services are purchases for which a consumer spends a lot of time shopping in order to compare prices, quality and style. Personal selling by the retailer is often a key factor in the purchase, particularly if the product is relatively complicated.
- Speciality goods and services are products that a consumer will make a special effort to locate.

As far as industrial products are concerned, two broad categories can be identified:

- Expense items are relatively inexpensive industrial products that are consumed within a year of their purchase.
- Capital items are relatively expensive industrial products that have a long life and are used in the operations of the business. Selecting capital items is often a long process and personal selling is often a key element in the purchasing decision.

Price

Once a company has developed a product it has to decide how to price it. This is a tricky decision and the stakes can be high. Before deciding on its pricing method the company has to define its objectives. Some of the most common are:

- to achieve a certain overall profit target
- to increase sales
- to get a bigger share of the market
- to achieve high profits on a particular product
- to discourage competition
- to promote a particular product image
- to accomplish social or ethical goals.

Promotion

Promotion is persuasive communication that motivates people to buy a company's products. It may take the form of advertising, personal selling, publicity, sales promotion, reseller support or a combination of these activities.

- **Advertising** is any paid form of impersonal presentation of goods, service or ideas using a mass communication medium.
- **Personal selling** is the use of person-to-person communication to assist or persuade a prospect to buy, and is used especially when the number of buyers is limited and the product is expensive and complicated. A good salesperson must have an intimate knowledge of the product and strategic understanding of the buyer.
- **Publicity** is unpaid media coverage of news about an organisation, its personnel or its products, Publicity may, of course, be positive or negative. Positive publicity may generate far more sales than pages of paid advertising.
- **Sales promotion** is a direct inducement that motivates someone to purchase a product. It covers a wide variety of activities such as exhibiting at trade shows, displaying material at a retail location, and giving away coupons that offer a discount.
- **Reseller support** refers to incentives given to wholesalers and retailers.

Place

There are many ways that products can be distributed to customers. The channel of distribution may include wholesalers, who sell products to other firms for resale or for industrial use, and retailers, who sell directly to the public. Here are a few examples of retail outlets:

- **department stores:** large stores that carry a wide variety of high-quality merchandise
- **speciality stores:** shops carrying only particular types of goods such as children's clothing
- **supermarkets:** large departmentalised stores specialising mainly in food and household products
- **mail order firms:** companies selling products through catalogues and shipping them directly to customers by mail
- **open-air markets, kiosks, trade shows, auctions.**

4.1.C
Discussion

The four Ps

1 Make a copy of the grid below and place the following products:

- a washing machine
- toothpaste
- an accountant
- paper clips
- a dry cleaner
- small components
- a Savile Row suit
- razor blades
- a hairdresser
- an Aston Martin
- a truck
- a medical specialist
- a robot
- a bed
- a meal at Maxim's in Paris
- an interior decorator
- janitorial services
- a Breitling watch

convenience goods	convenience services
shopping goods	**shopping services**
speciality goods	**speciality services**
expense items	**capital items**

2 In small groups, find other examples of products and place them in the above grid. Discuss three or four of the products, giving a description of the product, how it is packaged, where you can buy it, who buys it, how much it costs, what influences the buyer in his or her choice, etc.

3 Give an example of how personal selling has influenced a purchasing decision you have made.

4 Decide which form of promotion describes each of the activities in the grid below. Make a copy of the grid and fill it in by placing a ✓ in the appropriate boxes. Forms of promotion include:

- positive publicity
- negative publicity
- sales promotion
- reseller support.

	Positive publicity	Negative publicity	Sales promotion	Reseller support
a A newspaper article about our company's mineral water being polluted				
b A free display rack given to all supermarkets which display our products				
c A holiday for two for the winner of our "Wholesaler of the Year" competition				
d Local radio coverage of a sports event we organised				
e Free samples of our new product given to people in the street				

Can you think of any other examples of these forms of promotion?

5 Decide where you would go (either in your home country or abroad) to buy the following:

- white goods (fridge, freezer, hairdrier, etc)
- brown goods (hi-fi, television, radio, etc)
- fruit and vegetables
- clothes
- shoes
- a new car
- beauty products (make-up, perfume, after-shave lotion, etc)
- stationery (pens, paper, felt-tips, staples, etc)
- a can of soft drink.

6 Choose one retail outlet that you know well and discuss:

- its location
- the quality of its service
- its products
- other information of interest.

Vocabulary

Defining key terms

Match the following key terms with their definitions:

Terms

1	market segments	9	stock turnover
2	target markets	10	publicity
3	disposable personal income	11	trade show
4	product mix	12	point-of-purchase display
5	brand	13	couponing
6	generic products	14	wholesalers
7	trademark	15	retailers
8	market share	16	warehouse

Definitions

a Any name, sign or symbol used to identify the products of a firm.

b Products that bear only the name of the item, not of its producer, and which are sold at lower than normal prices.

c Proportion of the market controlled by a specific company or product.

d Facility for storing stocks of supplies or finished products.

e Distribution of certificates that entitle buyers to a discount on a particular item.

f Brand that has been given legal protection so that its owner has exclusive rights to its use.

g Industry gathering in which producers set up displays and demonstrate products to potential customers.

h Money that a family has to spend after paying taxes.

i Advertising or display materials set up at a retail location to encourage sales of an item.

j Firms that sell directly to the public.

k Groups of individuals or organisations within a market that share certain common characteristics.

l Specific groups of customers to whom a company wants to sell a particular product.

m Unpaid media coverage of news about an organisation.

n Firms that sell products to other firms for resale or for industrial use.

o Number of times that average inventory is sold during a given period.

p Complete list of all products that a company offers for sale.

Project

Developing a Marketing Mix

In small groups, choose three products with which you are familiar and develop a Marketing Mix for each of them. Make a copy of the grid below and fill it in. Give as much relevant information as possible regarding each element of the Marketing Mix.

	A convenience good or service	A speciality good or service	A capital item
Product			
Price			
Promotion			
Place			

Section 2
Interpreting marketing information

4.2.A
Analysis

Interpreting graphs

In small groups, study and discuss the following charts and graphs (Figures 7 to 9). Describe and analyse each one separately, then analyse any relationship between them.

Figure 7:
Shampoo products – market share 1991/92

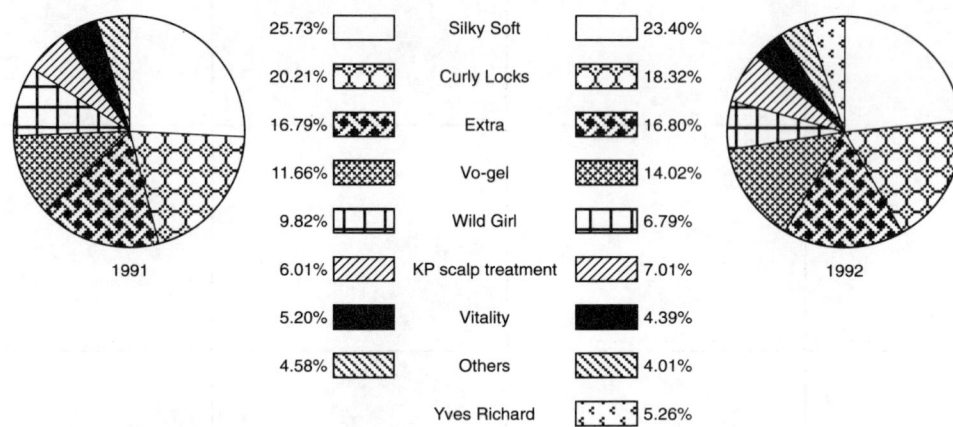

1991			1992
25.73%	Silky Soft	23.40%	
20.21%	Curly Locks	18.32%	
16.79%	Extra	16.80%	
11.66%	Vo-gel	14.02%	
9.82%	Wild Girl	6.79%	
6.01%	KP scalp treatment	7.01%	
5.20%	Vitality	4.39%	
4.58%	Others	4.01%	
	Yves Richard	5.26%	

Figure 8:
Silky Soft Shampoo – promotion budget (worldwide)

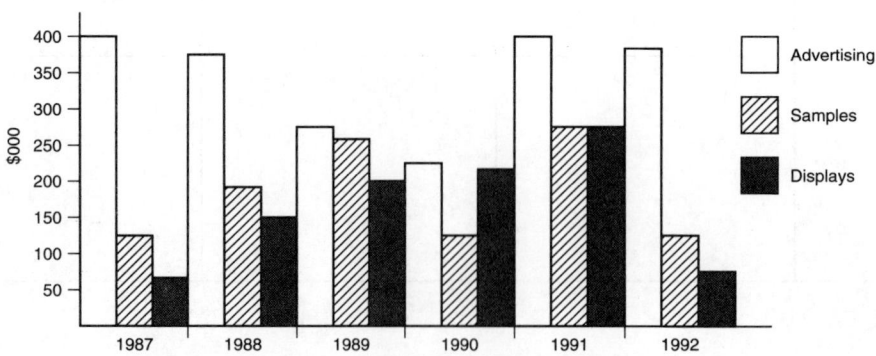

Figure 9:
Silky Soft Shampoo – sales

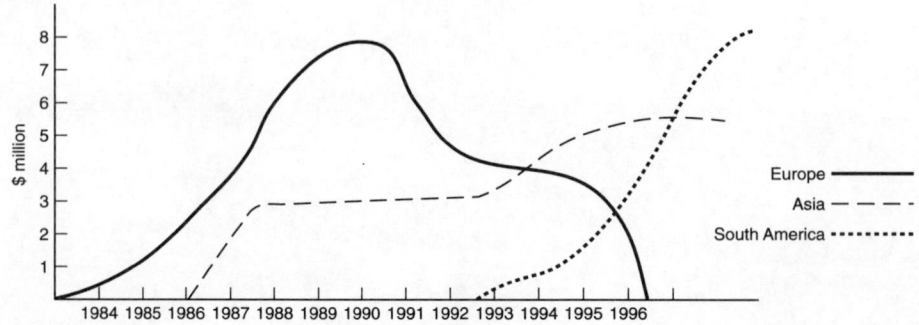

Quantities and trends

4.2.B
Word choice

1 Look again at Figures 7 to 9. Fill in the blanks in the following sentences. When you have finished, read them aloud.

1 Silky Soft's market share dropped _____ 25.73% _____ 23.40%

2 Curly Locks _____ an almost 2-point _____ .

3 Extra's market share remained _____ .

4 Vo-gel _____ a substantial increase in market share.

5 Wild Girl's market share dropped _____ .

6 Yves Richard _____ the market and _____ 5.26% of the market.

7 KP's market share rose _____ one percentage point.

8 Between 1987 and 1990, Silky Soft's advertising budget decreased _____ but in 1991 it rose _____ to $400,000.

9 A _____ of Silky Soft's promotion budget in 1992 was spent on samples.

10 There was a wild _____ in the budget for samples between 1989 and 1992.

11 Silky Soft's European Sales were _____ $4 million in 1986.

2 Discuss sales of Silky Soft Shampoo (Figure 9) again, using the following terms:

Example

> Silky Soft's European sales *reached* their *highest point* in 1989.

upward trend	downward trend
moved upwards	moved downwards
reached; amounted to; attained	declined; decreased; dwindled; fell;
growth; rise; upturn; upsurge	dropped; went down; slumped;
apex; zenith; highest point	plumetted; collapsed; slid; slipped

levelling off; turnaround	steeply; sharply;
launch; start up	dramatically
maturity	gradually;
shelf life	slowly; steadily
forecast	

4.2.C

Functions

Asking for and giving (or withholding) information

In pairs, use the following expressions to ask for and give (or withhold) information regarding the market for shampoo products and Silky Soft's promotion budget and sales.

Example

> A. 'I wonder if you could tell me whether the 1992 advertising budget was up or down on the previous year.'
> B. 'Yes, I've got the figures right in front of me. Advertising expenditure in 1992 was $380,000, down from $405,000 in 1991.'

Asking for information	**Giving (or withholding) information**
I wonder if you could tell me ...	Yes, I've got the figures right in front of me ...
I'd like to know ...	Sure, I'll just look that up for you ...
Could you let me have ...	According to my records ...
Could you tell me ...	I'm afraid this is classified information.
I'd like some information about ...	I'm sorry but I don't have that information available.

Section 3

Negotiating

4.3.A

Functions

Negotiating

Negotiating involves a number of language functions such as making proposals, inviting concessions and asking for clarification. Make a copy of the grid on page 55 and place the following sentences in the boxes (two sentences per box).

1   *I'm sorry, I didn't catch what you said.*
2   *I suggest that we fix the price at 870 deutchmarks per dozen.*
3   *I have no doubt that our customers will appreciate this product.*
4   *I can't go along with you/that.*
5   *If I were you I would take note of what your competitors are doing.*
6   *In return, we would hope that you extend the warranty to 3 years.*
7   *We were given to understand that labour charges were covered by the warranty.*
8   *That wouldn't be acceptable, I'm afraid.*
9   *That seems reasonable, I suppose.*
10 *What do you say we work on the basis of a 90 day payment period?*
11 *I'm afraid I'm not quite with you.*
12 *Have you thought of the advantages of leasing?*

13 *I'd like some more details about* your system of discounts.

14 *I think we could go along with that.*

15 *I really feel that* the packaging is too bright.

16 *If we did accept, we would expect you to* reciprocate by doubling the size of your order.

17 *Could you tell me some more about* your after-sales service?

18 *In other words,* I'm unable to improve upon my last offer.

19 *I'm rather surprised to see that* transport costs are not included in the price.

20 *What I mean is* that I'm not empowered to make that kind of decision.

Making proposals and counter-proposals	Reformulating information

Expressing opinions	Inviting a concession

Disagreeing	Asking for clarification

Querying	Asking for further information

Offering advice	Agreeing

Role play

Negotiation warm-up

Work in pairs. Agree upon a product (preferably an expense item, a capital item or a good for resale) and then prepare and carry out a very short negotiation based upon the following plan. Make full use of the expressions in exercise 4.3.A but do not allow yourself to be limited by them. Here are some examples of variables you may wish to negotiate.

---

higher discounts
cash payment
larger order
free delivery
more favourable terms of payment
annual loyalty rebate
shorter guarantee
longer guarantee
buyback/sale or return arrangement

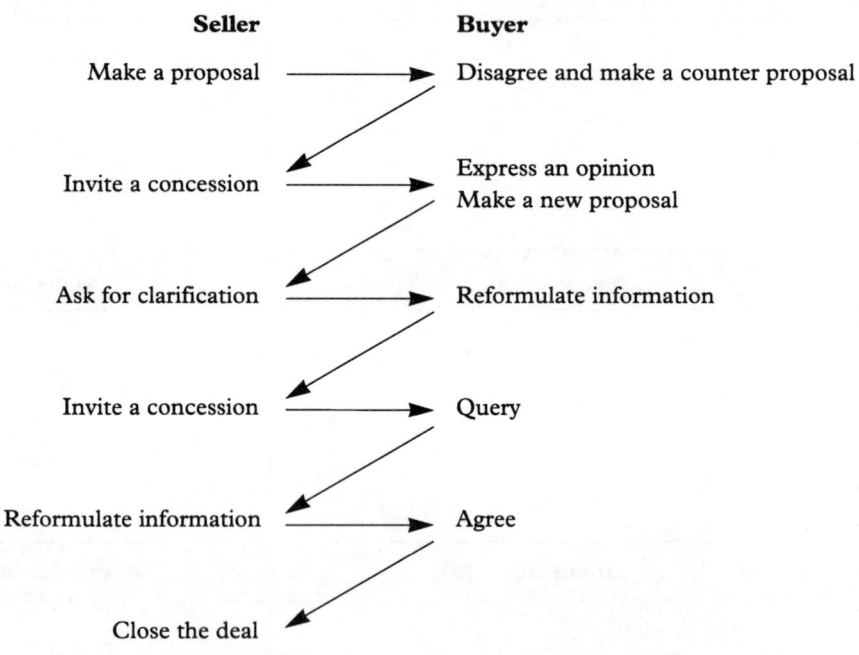

Seller	Buyer
Make a proposal	Disagree and make a counter proposal
Invite a concession	Express an opinion / Make a new proposal
Ask for clarification	Reformulate information
Invite a concession	Query
Reformulate information	Agree
Close the deal	

Example

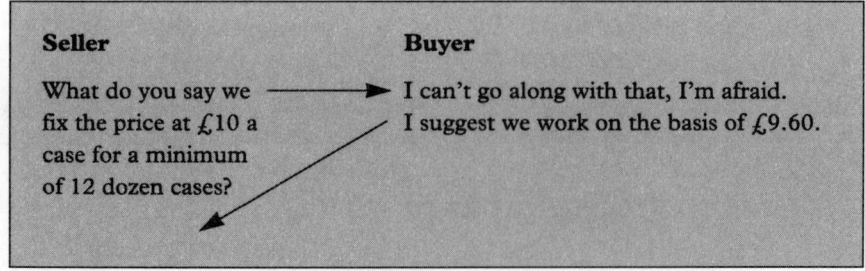

Seller	Buyer
What do you say we fix the price at £10 a case for a minimum of 12 dozen cases?	I can't go along with that, I'm afraid. I suggest we work on the basis of £9.60.

Change roles so that the buyer becomes the seller and vice versa. Choose a different product and carry out a negotiation following the above plan.

Negotiating a sale

Read the following information and then carry out the role play which follows.

Excalibur is an industrial robot produced by Axetti, a Franco-Italian engineering consortium. Rivalling the Japanese giants on price and performance, Excalibur has begun to carve a niche for itself in Europe's increasingly robotised manufacturing industries. Its main successes have been with small and medium-sized plants in two principal sectors: precision engineering and moulded plastics. British manufacturers, however, have been slow to invest and Axetti is desperately hoping to gain a foothold in Britain and build up a strong brand image before the Japanese monopolise the market. The company is also working on two new powerful models which are due to be launched within the next 18 months.

The engineering trade fair in Geneva last autumn was a good opportunity for Europe's industrialists to see Excalibur in action. One interested visitor was James Howell, Production Manager with an up-and-coming precision-tool manufacturer based in Coventry, England. On his return to Coventry Mr Howell spoke to his Managing Director, Pat Symes, about the need to invest in the most up-to-date technology if their company was to survive in a fiercely competitive environment.

Ms Symes did not need convincing. She had been looking closely at the rise of her new South-East Asian competitors with dismay and she also knew that Coventry's post-war economic downfall was mainly due to lack of investment. While Keil and Yokohama were modernising their plants in the fifties and sixties, Coventry sat back and watched. Ms Symes was determined not to make the same mistake as her father whose company went bankrupt while she was a teenager.

Mr Howell and Ms Symes flew out to Milan the following week to have a closer look at some of the ways Excalibur could be programmed to perform the various tasks needed for the production of precision tools. They also spent two afternoons with Axetti's Sales Director discussing prices, maintenance, training facilities and so on.

Three weeks later Ms Symes faxed a message to Axetti asking them to draw up a quotation for the purchase of four Excalibur industrial robots. Full robotisation of the Coventry plant would require 26 robots but Ms Symes felt it safer to restructure the production operations in stages.

This is a summary of the quotation drawn up by Axetti.

Figure 10:
Axetti's quotation

QUOTATION

£148,000

Quantity	4 Excalibur robots @ £37,000
Delivery date	6 months after ordering
Terms of payment	20% of invoice amount on ordering
	30% of invoice amount on receipt of order
	50% of invoice amount within 90 days of receipt of order
Training	4 day training programme for 10 robot operators and maintenance personnel on **£18,000**
	Axetti premises in Milan (accommodation and meals included)
Warranty	*Axetti undertakes to repair or replace any faulty component for a period of 12 months from receipt of order. Labour costs and cost of components will be met by Axetti provided that the damage is not due to negligence or accident.*

In pairs, read the role cards that have been assigned to you and negotiate an agreement that gives you the best possible deal.

Remember a negotiation differs from a simple sale insofar as a negotiation often involves several variables, for example:

- price
- discounts
- delivery date
- delivery point
- guarantee provisions
- sale or return arrangements.

- length of guarantee
- training facilities
- after-sales service
- supply of spare parts
- buy-back arrangement

A skilful negotiator will:

- Try and obtain his or her opponent's list of variables before the negotiation begins.
- Keep in mind all the variables at all times.
- Not be afraid of introducing new variables whenever necessary. Everything is negotiable!
- Trade off one variable against another. A skilful negotiator will never *donate* a concession but will 'trade concessions' so that something conceded is matched by something gained.
- Aim high but be prepared to compromise. If you do not aim high at the beginning you cannot raise the stakes later on.
- Finish the negotiation with both sides feeling satisfied with the outcome. This is essential if a long-term relationship is to be built.

Axetti's role card

Your robots are just right for Pat Symes's company. She knows this and she also knows that you know this. You will therefore have a psychological advantage at the forthcoming negotiation. On the other hand Ms Symes must know how much you want to enter the British market. In some ways the Coventry plant will be you showroom in Britain and a prominent customer will provide a good springboard for your new products.

Axetti has recently developed a leasing arrangement whereby customers can hire robots with an option to buy. You have not yet mentioned this to Ms Symes as you would prefer to make a cash sale at this stage.

Do not be afraid of introducing new variables into the negotiation. Remember to try and obtain Ms Symes's list of variables before the negotiation begins. She is going to negotiate hard so try and find ways of obtaining concessions in exchange for those you give.

Pat Symes's role card

Although you recognise Excalibur's qualities you are not satisfied with Axetti's quotation as it stands and wish to negotiate every point. You are also worried about Axetti's after-sales service and would like further details. For example, is there a 24-hour breakdown service or will you have to wait three months for repairs to be carried out? Another source of concern is whether or not Axetti operate a buy-back arrangement whereby they will take back ageing robots at a future date at a guaranteed price.

4.3.D
Vocabulary

Verbs and nouns in context

I Fill in the blanks in the following paragraph using verbs from the list below, and conjugating them where necessary.

accomplish	infringe
quote	promote
place	launch
break into	reap
carve	strike

We wanted to _____ 1 _____ the SE Asian market by _____ 2 _____ a new product, _____ 3 _____ a strong brand image, and _____ 4 _____ a niche for ourselves before our competitors arrived. In order to _____ 5 _____ our goals, we _____ 6 _____ a deal with a Korean importer who agreed to the price we had _____ 7 _____ and _____ 8 _____ an immediate order for 10,000 units. If we can extend our activities to some of the neighbouring countries, we should be able to _____ 9 _____ huge benefits, but we will have to be careful if we are to avoid _____ 10 _____ import regulations.

2 Find the nouns which correspond to the following verbs.

Example

to motivate → motivation

1	to accomplish	11	to display
2	to quote	12	to distribute
3	to infringe	13	to specialise
4	to promote	14	to sample
5	to present	15	to sell
6	to persuade	16	to cover
7	to purchase	17	to analyse
8	to induce	18	to relate
9	to know	19	to rise
10	to exhibit	20	to suggest

3 Write a short paragraph using five of the nouns from the exercise above.

UNIT 5
Promotion

Advertising

Types of advertising

Read the following passage then work on exercise 5.1.B.

Advertising may be classified according to which of three promotional goals it is designed to reach:

- **Generic advertising** attempts to raise demand for a particular product regardless of brand.
- **Brand advertising** aims at increasing sales of a particular brand and accounts for most of the money spent globally on advertising.
- **Institutional advertising** or *corporate advertising*, tries to build a certain image for an organisation and thus create goodwill rather than sell specific products. A subcategory of institutional advertising is *advocacy advertising* which addresses hotly debated public issues.

An advertising campaign can only be designed when the following questions have been answered:

- what are the organisation's objectives?
- who is the target audience?
- how much should the organisation allocate to the campaign?
- what creative appeal should be used?
- which medium is the most appropriate?

Numerous scientific studies in the United States have yielded guidelines for creating advertisements with impact. These guidelines, however, differ from medium to medium, as can be seen from the summaries which follow.

Three types of advertising

Work in small groups.

1 Find an example of each of the three types of advertising (generic, brand and institutional). Describe the advertisements and point out any differences in style.

2 The guidelines on page 61 were designed for the American media and American audiences. Are there any points you would change if you were to advise companies or organisations on how to advertise in your country?

WHAT WORKS BEST IN PRINT

1. *Get your message in the headline.* The headline should tell the whole story – including the brand name and the key consumer promise. Research shows that four out of five readers do not get further than the headline. If you depend on the body copy to tell your story, you are wasting 80 per cent of your money.

2. *Use the headline to grab your prospect.* If the ad is directed toward a special group, single out those prospects in the headline. Appeal to their self-interest.

3. *Offer a benefit in the headline.* Headlines that promise a benefit sell more than those that don't. Reader's Digest, which employs some of the best headline writers in the business, has three guiding principles for headlines: Present a benefit to the reader. Make the benefit quickly apparent. Make the benefit easy to get.

4. *Inject new into your headline.* Your product will be new only once. If you have a new product, or an improvement on an existing product, announce it with a loud bang.

5. *Don't be afraid of long headlines.* Research shows that, on the average, long headlines sell more merchandise than short ones.

6. *Avoid negative headlines.* People are literal-minded and may remember only the negative. Sell the positive benefits of your product – not the fact that it won't harm or that some defect has been solved. Look for emotional words that attract and motivate, like free and love.

7. *Look for story appeal in your illustration.* Next to the headline, an illustration is the most effective way to get a reader's attention. Try for story appeal, the kind of illustration that makes the reader ask: "What's going on here?"

8. *Use photographs.* Research shows that photography increases recall an average of 26 per cent over drawings.

9. *Use before-and-after photographs.* They make a point better than words. If you can, show a visual contract – a change in the consumer or a demonstration of product superiority.

10. *Use simple layouts.* One big picture works better than several small ones. Avoid cluttered pages. Layouts that resemble the magazine's editorial format are likely to be read.

11. *Don't be afraid of long copy.* The people who read beyond the headline are prospects for your product If your product is expensive – like a car, a vacation, or an industrial program – prospects are hungry for the information that long copy gives them. And write the copy the way people actually talk.

12. *Use testimonials.* They add believability. As in television, endorsements by real people are memorable and persuasive.

WHAT WORKS BEST IN TELEVISION

1. *Let the picture tell the story.* Television is a visual medium. That's why the people in front of the set are called viewers. They remember what they see, not what they hear.

2. *Look for a "key" visual.* A commercial with many different scenes may look interesting, but it may turn out to be overcomplicated. Busy, crowded, fast-moving commercials are hard to understand.

3. *Grab the viewer's attention.* Analysis of audience reaction shows either a sharp drop or a sharp rise in interest during the first five seconds. After that, the audience can only become less interested, never more. So offer the viewer something right off the bat: news, a problem you have the solution to, a conflict that is involving.

4. *Be single-minded.* A good commercial is uncomplicated and direct. It never makes the viewer do a lot of mental work. The basic length of a television commercial in the United States is 30 seconds. The content possible in that time is outlined in the phrase "name-claim-demonstration": the name of your product, your consumer benefit, and the reason the consumer should believe it.

5. *Show people, not objects.* People are interested in people. You will have a more memorable commercial – and register more key points – if you show a person on-camera with the product instead of the product in limbo with a voice coming from off-screen.

6. *Provide a payoff.* Show that the product does what you said it will – a "moment of affirmation". At some point, the homemaker should admire the whiter wash, the shaver should stroke his smooth cheek, the dog should eat the dog food.

WHAT WORKS BEST IN RADIO

1. *Stretch the listener's imagination.* Voices and sounds can evoke pictures.

2. *Listen for a memorable sound.* What will make your commercial stand out from the clutter? A distinctive voice, a memorable jingle, a solution to the listener's problem.

3. *Present one idea.* It is difficult to communicate more than one idea in a television commercial. In radio, which is subject to more distractions, it is nearly impossible. Be direct and clear.

4. *Select your audience quickly.* It pays to attract your segment of the audience at the beginning of the commercial – before they can switch to another station.

5. *Mention your brand name and your promise early.* Audiences are more aware of commercials that do so. Mentioning the band name and promise more than once also heightens awareness.

6. *Use music.* Music is particularly helpful in reaching teenagers, who prefer the "new sounds" offered by music stations. You can give our campaign infinite variety with the same lyrics arranged in different ways and sung by different people.

7. *Ask listeners to take action.* People respond to radio requests for action. Don't be afraid to ask listeners to call now, write in, or send money.

8. *Use the strength of radio personalities.* Consider commercials delivered live instead of recorded ones. Many local disc jockeys and personalities have strong hold on their audiences. If they believe in your product, they can sell it better than you can.

5.1.C
Vocabulary

Defining key terms

1 Match the following key terms with the definitions which follow.

Terms	**Definitions**
1 brochure	**a** time when television or radio audiences are greatest
2 broadsheet	**b** a promotional gift
3 tabloid	**c** the final customer
4 colour supplement	**d** size of audience reached by an advertisement
5 flier	**e** a small promotional leaflet
6 freesheet	**f** broadcasting time
7 freebie	**g** shiny and attractive
8 periodical	**h** a magazine which accompanies a newspaper
9 pamphlet	**i** a newspaper financed entirely by adverts
10 prospectus	**j** a large-sized newspaper
11 billboard	**k** the number of people who read a publication
12 air time	**l** a thin booklet with a paper cover
13 prime time	**m** a company's design put on its products and possessions
14 caption	**n** a very short text accompanying a picture
15 jingle	**o** visiting potential customers
16 canvassing	**p** the main text of an advertisement
17 copy	**q** a specialised journal published regularly
18 end user	**r** an illustrated booklet for advertising products
19 livery	**s** a simple tune to advertise a product
20 leadership	**t** an information document produced by a school, university or company
21 exposure	**u** a small-sized newspaper
22 glossy	**v** an outdoor site where large advertisements are posted

2 Classify the terms under these headings:

- print media
- broadcasting media
- others

5.1.D
Project

Analysing an advertisement

Choose an advertisement (generic, brand or institutional) and, if possible, bring a copy of it or a recording of it to class. In a five-minute oral presentation try to cover the following points:

- describe the advertisement
- who is it aimed at?
- what is it trying to achieve?
- how is it trying to achieve its goals?
- why do you think this media vehicle was chosen?
- does the advertisement respect the guidelines as defined in exercise 5.1.A for the American market?
- do you think the advertisement succeeds?

Do you know whether your advertisement is part of a broader campaign? If so, explain what else the company or organisation is doing.

Listening

How an advertising budget is established

Listen to the tape recording of an extract from a lecture on how an advertising budget is established. Copy the grid below on to your own paper and fill it in as you listen to the tape.

Method	Budget based on	Strengths	Weaknesses
1			
2			
3			
4			

1 What type of business might use the first method and why?

2 List four advertising objectives mentioned in the lecture.

The media

5.2.A
Discussion and reading

The pros and cons of the media

I In small groups, discuss the pros and cons of the major advertising media from the advertiser's point of view. Copy the grid below on to your own paper and fill in with your own ideas.

Medium	Advantages	Disadvantages
Newspaper		
Television		
Direct mail		
Radio		
Magazine		

When you have finished, read the text on the following page and add any new points to your grid.

The pros and cons of the major advertising media

There are many different ways in which an advertiser's message can be communicated to his or her audience. In the States, as well as most other developed countries, newspapers still attract the largest share of the total advertising budget, with television, radio, direct mail and magazines accounting for most of the rest. Other media such as billboards, yellow pages, videotex and telemarketing, although growing steadily, still account for a relatively small part of the amount spent on advertising. Each medium, of course, has its own strengths and weaknesses, and a prospective advertiser would do well to consider these when devising the company's advertising strategy.

The main advantage of newspaper advertising is its broad reach, getting through to a wide spectrum of the population. There's a permanence which you don't have with the electronic media and an all-year-round readership which makes long-term strategies feasible. Regional newspapers also offer the advantages of geographical selectivity and flexibility. On the other hand, newspapers usually don't offer colour, and if they do the availability is limited and very often of mediocre quality. Most newspapers offer little in the way of demographic selectivity, which can make precise targeting very tricky.

Television's main appeal is that it offers a combination of sight and sound, which opens up an almost infinite range of creative possibilities. Furthermore, messages can be broadcast very frequently and, like newspapers, to a very broad target. The chief disadvantage, of course, is the high cost of production and air time. The message tends to be short-lived and is often not seen at all as many viewers now have VCRs and skip over the advertisements.

Direct mail campaigns or mail shots as they're otherwise known, rely on mailing lists containing the names of likely prospects. Obviously, the more specific the list, the more effective the campaign is likely to be – and some lists are *very* specific; for example, a list might contain the names of all the female shareholders between the ages of 40 and 65 in a particular geographical area and this makes targeting specific prospects much easier. Direct mail also has the ability to saturate a specific area quickly using a style and format that offers enormous flexibility. On the minus side, however, direct mail often meets with a certain amount of consumer resistance. It's also relatively expensive per exposure.

Radio offers the advantages of low cost and large potential audience. As with television, advertisers can select the stations and times favoured by the audience they want to reach but, like television viewers, listeners can easily switch stations when the advertisements come on. Even if they don't switch stations, there's a tendency for people to use the radio for background sound and ignore the advertisments. Maybe it's because radio doesn't offer any visual possibilities.

Magazines differ from newspapers in several respects. Firstly, they tend to be kept much longer, sometimes for several weeks or months, and are often passed from person to person. Secondly, the quality of the reproduction is much better, which means advertisers can show their products accurately and create a quality image. Thirdly, special interest magazines offer greater selectivity in reaching specific market segments. However, the costs tend to be high and the campaign usually has to be prepared a long time in advance.

2 Work in small groups and discuss which media would be used to promote the following in your own countries:

- a local clothes shop
- a car
- cigarettes
- a computer
- a language course
- an insurance policy
- furniture
- alcohol
- road safety campaigns
- funeral services
- weapons
- political parties

Why are these media, rather than others, used?

Making suggestions, justifying, agreeing and disagreeing

1 Imagine you are at a brainstorming session to look at ways of boosting your company's sales. Make suggestions by completing the sentences below using the correct verb form. Vary your verbs as much as possible.

Example

> Launch (verb)
> Landing (verb + ing)
> To launch (to + verb)

1 I think we ought ...
2 Surely we should ...
3 I suggest we ...
4 I suggest ...
5 How about ...
6 One possibility would be ...
7 It might be a good idea ...
8 Let's ...
9 We could perhaps ...
10 It might be worth ...
11 Why don't we ...
12 Why not ...
13 I would recommend that we ...
14 I would recommend ...
15 What if we ...

2 In small groups, decide on a product then suggest which media might be used to promote it. Use the expressions given above as much as possible. Each time you make a suggestion, justify it.

Example

> Why don't we place a series of full-page ads in *The Sun*? Their readership is over seven million and we'd get maximum exposure.

Repeat the exercise. Each time somebody makes a suggestion, agree or disagree using one of the following expressions, then justify your decision.

Example

> **A** Why don't we place a series of full-page ads in *The Sun*? Their readership is over seven million and we'd get maximum exposure.
> **B** That may be so but *The Sun* really doesn't correspond to the image of quality we're trying to project.
> **C** I feel the same way. We're aiming at a thinking public, the kind that might read *The Guardian* or *The Independent*.

Agreeing	**Disagreeing**
I totally agree.	I can't go along with that.
I feel the same way.	I can't go along with you.
That's exactly what I feel.	That wouldn't be acceptable.
I think you have a good point.	That's out of the question.
You may have something there.	I'm afraid I can't accept that.
I'd go along with that.	I'm afraid I can't agree with you.
It seems reasonable to me.	That might be so but ...
	Yes, but the trouble is that ...

Section 3

Campaigns

Which media do they choose?

Table 4 on pages 68 and 69 represents the main advertisers in the French media in 1991. Read aloud the gross investment figures. In small groups, analyse the main trends which the figures reveal and explain the possible reasons for these trends. Report your findings to the class.

Example

> Cinema advertising is dominated by ads for tobacco and alcohol. This may be due to legislation which restricts advertising such products in many other media. Also, the cinema attracts a young audience which represents a major target for cigarette and alcohol producers.

The following verbs and expressions may be useful:

- to spend
- to attract
- to dominate

- to restrict
- to advertise
- to be present

- to aim at
- to spread
- to concentrate

- this may be due to ...
- the reason for this may be ...
- this could be explained by ...

The following abbreviations are used in the table:

Auto: automobile
ret: retailing
gamb: gambling
TC: Telecommunications
cos: cosmetics
tob: tobacco
alc: alcohol

comp: computers
elec: electronics
ener: energy
ins: insurance
chem: chemicals
SC: soap/cosmetics

Table 4:
The main advertisers in the French media in 1991

WHICH MEDIA DO THEY CHOOSE?			
Daily newspapers			
Company	Industry	Gross investment in 000 FF	% of company's total advertising expenditure
1 Renault	auto	258 187	29.5
2 Casino	ret	222 479	54.2
3 Leclerc	ret	191 818	60.7
4 France Loto	gamb	173 096	42.6
5 Cora	ret	166 164	76.8
6 Peugeot	auto	133 752	21.6
7 Citroën	auto	117 776	26.9
8 Auchan	ret	114 903	44.5
9 Système U	ret	101 503	59.5
10 Intermarché	ret	95 700	46.6
Magazines			
1 France Télécom	TC	146 750	50.4
2 Renault	auto	146 404	16.8
3 VAG	auto	129 371	19.9
4 Peugeot	auto	95 644	15.4
5 Guerlain	cos	86 473	87.4
6 Seita	tob	86 722	68.2
7 Nestlé	food	78 836	18.3
8 Christian Dior	cos	78 359	72.2
9 Rover	auto	70 704	39.8
10 Moët Hennessy	alc	67 513	68.1
Specialised reviews			
1 France Télécom	TC	9 348	3.2
2 IBM	comp	7 960	11.3
3 Canon	elec	4 959	4.6
4 Crédit Agricole	bank	4 708	3.3
5 Electricité de France	ener	3 722	3.7
6 Société Générale	bank	3 359	4.8
7 Sony	elec	3 195	4.6
8 UAP	ins	2 645	2.8
9 Peugeot	auto	2 329	0.4
10 Philips	elec	2 160	0.1

Television

1	Henkel	chem	376 586	84.8
2	Procter & Gamble	SC	343 997	93.4
3	Nestlé	food	276 303	64.1
4	Gervais-Danone	food	265 959	94.7
5	Palmolive	SC	247 312	79.1
6	Lever	food	210 133	80.4
7	Peugeot	auto	202 212	32.7
8	L'Oréal	cos	161 381	72.0
9	Unisabi	food	156 233	69.7
10	Renault	auto	149 175	17.1

Radio

1	VAG	auto	142 252	21.9
2	But	ret	138 019	53.0
3	Renault	auto	122 087	14.0
4	Continent	ret	105 728	63.9
5	Peugeot	auto	104 198	16.8
6	Ford	auto	101 688	33.6
7	Conforama	ret	92 427	37.2
8	Fiat	auto	85 964	25.6
9	Intermarché	ret	83 227	40.5
10	Casino	ret	79 809	19.5

Billboards

1	VAG	auto	207 102	31.9
2	Renault	auto	189 095	21.6
3	Leclerc	ret	110 262	34.9
4	Auchan	ret	106 388	41.2
5	France Loto	gamb	97 381	24.0
6	Fiat	auto	88 555	26.4
7	Peugeot	auto	80 998	13.1
8	Casino	ret	73 526	17.9
9	Conforama	ret	69 430	27.9
10	Française de Brasserie	alc	63 022	43.0

Cinema

1	Seita	tob	31 025	24.5
2	Peter Stuyvesant	tob	26 100	42.5
3	Reynolds	tob	24 481	26.6
4	Philips	elec	22 249	9.9
5	Marlboro	tob	22 000	38.4
6	Nestlé	food	19 029	4.4
7	Ricard	alc	16 639	24.1
8	Française de Brasserie	alc	12 654	8.6
9	Moët Hennessy	alc	12 203	12.3
10	Kronenbourg	alc	11 966	8.7

Discussion

Describing and analysing graphs

In pairs, describe and analyse the graphs in Figure 11. What explanations can you give for these seasonal variations? Why would an advertiser be interested in data of this kind?

Figure 11:
French television viewing data

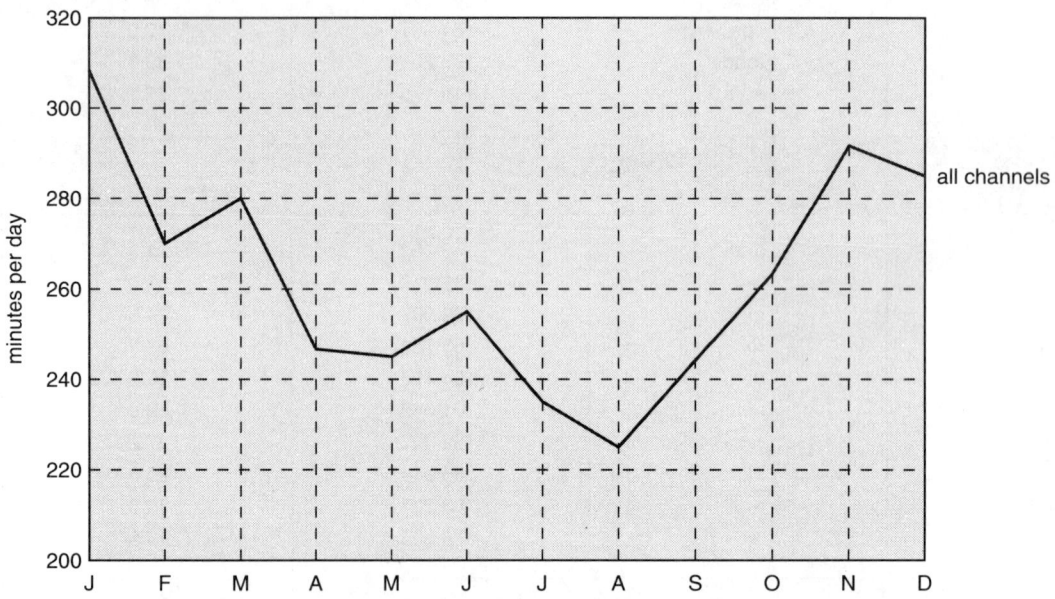

Seasonal variations in French television audiences

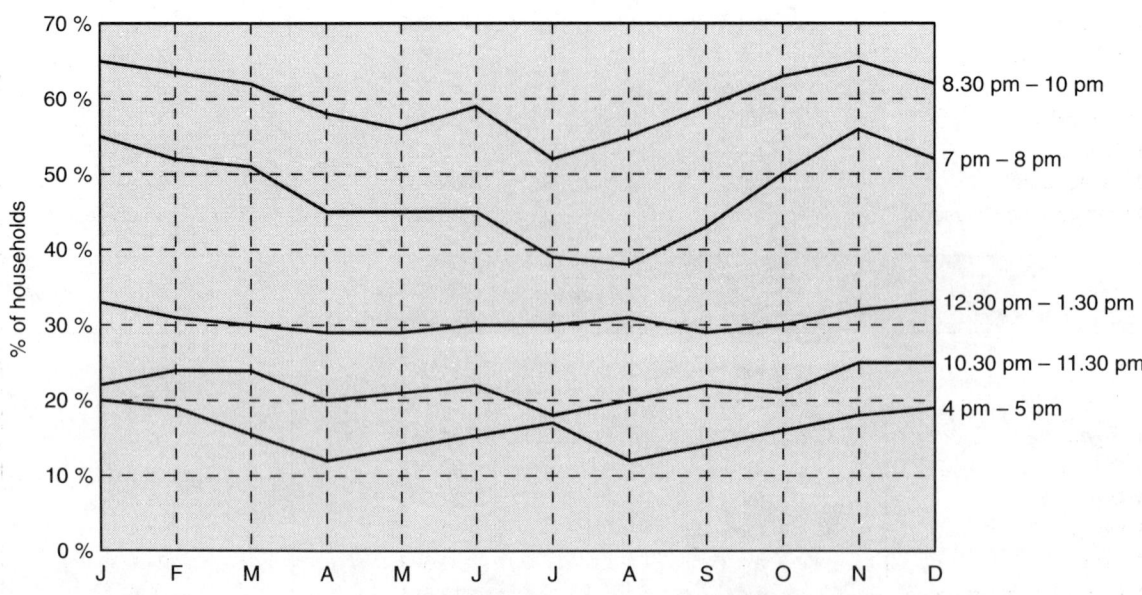

Seasonal variations in French television audiences according to the time of day

Compound words

1 Match each of the words in the first column with words in the second column to make compound nouns.

1	market	**a**	segment
2	market	**b**	tuners
3	disposable	**c**	material
4	pie	**d**	income
5	department	**e**	channel
6	life	**f**	loyalty
7	pocket	**g**	agency
8	stereo	**h**	transport
9	burglar	**i**	cleaners
10	vacuum	**j**	ovens
11	microwave	**k**	calculators
12	brand	**l**	share
13	cash	**m**	window
14	mass	**n**	pending
15	advertising	**o**	chart
16	trade	**p**	power
17	distribution	**q**	media
18	raw	**r**	margin
19	farm	**s**	show
20	air	**t**	alarms
21	profit	**u**	store
22	telephone	**v**	produce
23	purchasing	**w**	discount
24	patent	**x**	directory
25	shop	**y**	cycle

2 Write a concise definition for five of the above compound nouns *without using a dictionary*. In small groups, read your definitions without using the words that make up the compound nouns. The other members of your group have to find the compound noun you are defining.

3 Simplify the words in italics in the following sentences by using compound words.

1) We'll place an advertisement in the *press which specialises in horse-racing.*
2) The Italian *market for wines* is growing.
3) *Shoes for basketball* represent an expanding market.
4) We'll need *the support of advertising.*
5) We may have to change the design on the *pots in which yoghurt is sold.*

5.3.D
Project

Creating an advertising campaign

Imagine your company is developing a product (a good or a service) which you hope to launch in one year's time. The Marketing Director has called a meeting in order to develop an appropriate advertising campaign.

In small groups, appoint someone to role play the Marketing Director. He or she will steer the discussion and, after the meeting, will report back the following information to the class:

- the nature of the product
- the company's objectives
- the financial constraints
- the target audience
- the creative appeal
- the most appropriate medium or media.

The Marketing Director will be expected to justify each point, answer any question raised by the class and give as many details as possible within the time constraint imposed by the teacher.

5.3.E
Writing

A business report

Imagine you are the Marketing Director for an overseas subsidiary of an American multinational. Your company is developing one of the following products which you hope to launch in one year's time:

- a new-formula toothpaste with battery-operated dispenser
- a rapid ice-cube maker
- a pocket-size electronic encyclopaedia
- an anti-wrinkle face lotion
- a zero-cholesterol, zero-sugar chocolate bar which actually helps you lose weight
- an alcohol-free beer
- a rechargeable electric screwdriver
- a low-risk, high-yield investment scheme
- a combined leisure and commercial centre.

Write a report to Head Office.

The objectives of your report are as follows:

- To **inform** Head Office of your project. You will need to *describe* the four Ps of the Marketing Mix and *justify* each element wherever appropriate.
- To **describe** key elements of the campaign including timing, costs and personnel.
- To **convince** Head Office of the importance and value of your project. You need to gain their support if the campaign is to go ahead.

The report should not exceed four pages and should, if possible, be typewritten and double-spaced with 2.5cm margins. If necessary, refer to the guidelines on report writing in exercise 3.2.D (page 38).

UNIT 6
Retailing and merchandising

Section 1

Merchandising

6.1.A
Reading

Retailing and merchandising

Read the following passage and complete the true/false exercise which follows.

The post-war period has seen a radical change in the nature of retailing in many advanced industrialised countries. An overbundance of small shops which bought and sold on a small scale and relied heavily on personal service for their success, has given way to an increasing concentration of large specialised stores and retail chains with highly sophisticated logistical support systems and well-differentiated positioning strategies.

Increasing concentration has been accompanied by a reduction in the number of retail outlets as many shops have failed to keep pace with the competition. Producers have had to deal more and more with highly rationalised central purchasing offices where the retailer's negotiating powers have become immense. A direct consequence of this is that producers have had to drastically reduce their sales force and concentrate more on other marketing techniques such as interactive merchandising in order to win shelf space.

Until the 1960s, merchandising was relatively unimportant because the customer was rarely in direct contact with the product in the shop. A counter and a sales assistant usually kept them apart. With the development of self-service retail outlets, however, the product needed to be able to sell itself, hence the growing importance of merchandising. We can define merchandising as *'the marketing techniques used to present the product in the most favourable conditions, both materially and psychologically'*. It involves an active presentation in which the packaging and visual display of the product are paramount.

From the producer's point of view, merchandising is a key point in negotiating shelf space with retailers, and a way of maximising sales. The producer's merchandisers must ensure that, once accepted by the retailer, their products are well-presented on the shelves and there is no danger of the retailer running out of stock.

From the retailer's point of view, merchandising is a way of optimising shelf-space and maximising its profitability. He or she must constantly review the mix of products being presented, their location in the store and on the shelves, the amount of space given to each product, their price, promotions and so on. Above all, the design of the store should encourage the movement of customers into every part so that 'what can be seen may be handled, and what can be handled may be bought'. Placing high-turnover items in various parts of the store and signposting them clearly is one way of achieving this.

Store design should also take into account the nature of each product, so that items whose purchase needs some reflection should be given more space than items which are bought on impulse. Another consideration is the height at which products are presented.

Levels 3 and 4 are at eye-level and are therefore the most attractive. Level 2, at hand-level, is reasonably attractive but Level 1 is much less so. Level 5 may be attractive if it is not too high. The customer associates Level 1 with low-priced

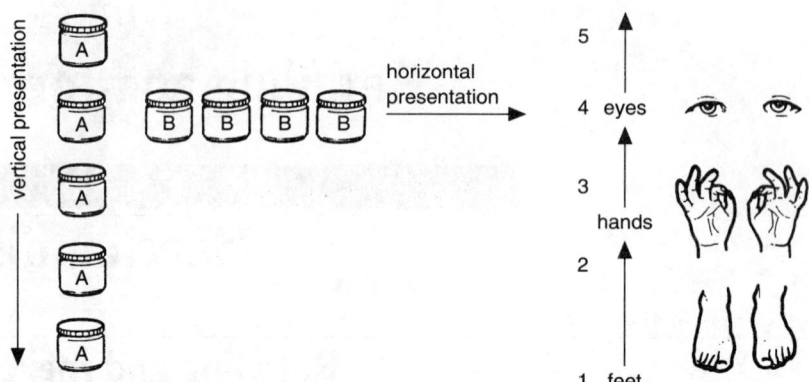

products or basic products, whereas Levels 4 and 5 are associated with more sophisticated, up-market items.

There is a golden rule which says that 'mass attracts'. Two methods are used to achieve this:

- vertical presentation, whereby different families of one product are grouped together
- horizontal presentation, whereby different brands of one family are grouped together.

Although offering a wide range of products tends to stimulate customers into buying impulse items such as biscuits and crisps, this is not the case for basic products such as flour and sugar where the variety of products has practically no effect on overall sales. Furthermore, too much diversification on any one shelf may confuse the customer who may not find what he or she is looking for and end up buying nothing.

The proximity of a particular product to a product leader may also be of importance, although there are differing views on this. In some cases, being in close proximity to a leading brand may lead to significant loss of sales, especially if the product belongs to the same segment as the leader. On the other hand, some products may reap the benefits of synergy by being placed close to a leader. It is important to remember that there are no absolute rules which can be applied to all stores at all times, but only recommendations which can be made. Each store tends to develop its own merchandising philosophy in keeping with its conception of the market and its overall strategy.

Say whether the following statements are true or false by marking with a ✓. Justify your answers.

	True	False
1 Nowadays, retailing relies more on personal service than it did in the past.	☐	☐
2 Retailers are becoming fewer and fewer.	☐	☐
3 By grouping together all the high-turnover products, the retailer will maximise sales.	☐	☐
4 The distance between shelves should always be the same.	☐	☐
5 Supermarkets usually offer a limited range of sugar because greater selection would not mean greater sales.	☐	☐
6 The producer's merchandisers rarely visit the stores which stock their products.	☐	☐

6.1.B

Grammar

Linking cause and effect

Use the following link words to compose sentences which preserve the cause and effect relationships below. Transform structures whenever necessary.

has led to	has brought about	(as) a result of
has caused	due to	the consequence of
has meant	owing to	has arisen from
has enabled	because of	has come about with

Example

Cause	Effect
increasing concentration of retailers	producers more dependent

> *An increasing concentration of retailers has led to producers becoming more dependent.*
> or
> *As a result of the increasing concentration of retailers, producers have become more dependent.*

	Cause	Effect
1	Retailers group together to negotiate purchases	producers have to reduce sales force
2	Retailers employ highly trained purchasers	producers have to employ highly trained salesmen
3	Retailers develop own generic brands	producers have to compete with retailers
4	Retailers develop sophisticated logistics	producers now deal with fewer delivery points
5	The development of self-service	products need to sell themselves
6	Failure to keep pace with competition	reduction in the number of retail outlets
7	Customers have direct contact with products	growing importance of merchandising
8	The spread of the automobile	retailers locate on the outskirts of town

6.1.C
Vocabulary

Fill in the blanks

Fill in each blank with an appropriate term from the following list:

> retail chains
> central purchasing offices
> shelf space
> counter
> signposting
> check-out desk
> aisles
> display racks
> trolley
> DIY

1 _____ are used at strategic points in order to diversify the presentation and stimulate sales.

2 It can be a long and expensive process to win _____ in a hypermarket.

3 Marks and Spencer is one of Britain's largest _____ .

4 Please pay at the _____ .

5 At a supermarket you put your shopping in a _____ .

6 You can find nails and screws in our _____ section.

7 Producers no longer deal with individual retailers but with powerful _____ .

8 An efficient system of _____ in the main _____ encourages the flow of customers.

9 Buying goods over the _____ will soon be a thing of the past.

6.1.D
Listening

The layout of a supermarket

1 Listen to a supermarket manager describe the layout of his supermarket. Label the numbered areas on Figure 12.

2 In which way does the layout of this supermarket help to:

● optimise sales?
● simplify restocking the shelves?
● minimise cash desk irregularities?

Figure 12:
The layout of a supermarket

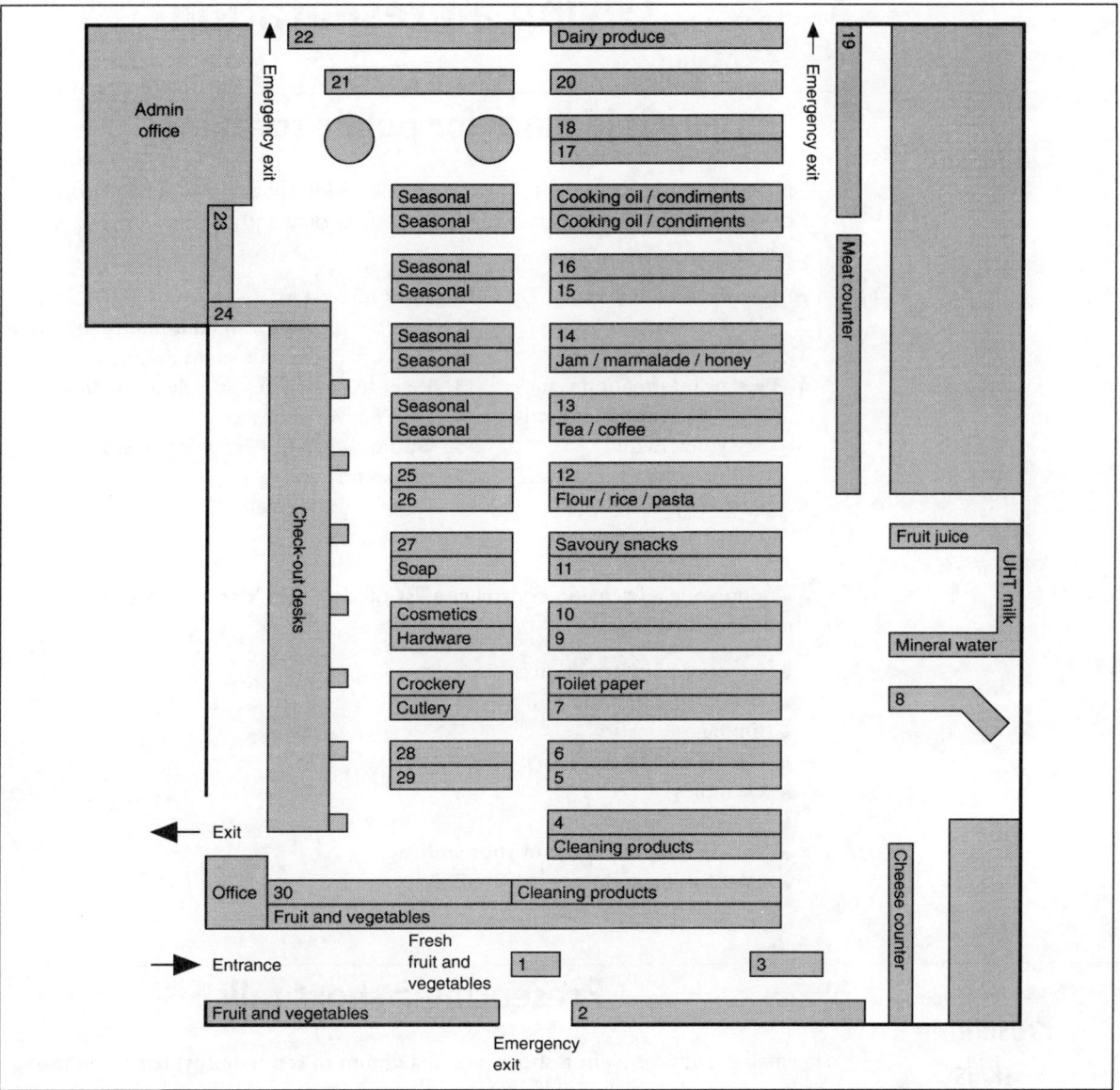

3 In pairs, choose one of the following rows or counters and list all the products you would expect to find there:

- cleaning products
- fish counter
- savoury snacks
- dairy products
- crockery.

4 Discuss with a partner the following questions:

Is there a natural progression from one product to another in this supermarket? Would you make any changes in the layout?

5 What other factors are important to customers that might affect their loyalty to the shop?

Section 2
Giving a presentation

6.2.A
Discussion

Guidelines for public speaking

I In small groups rank the following guidelines for speaking in public in order of importance. Be prepared to justify your choice and to offer any related advice.

1 Use short sentences.
2 Ask rhetorical questions.
3 Avoid negatives.
4 Present information visually.
5 Speak clearly and correctly.
6 Vary your rhythm.
7 Modulate your intonation.
8 Pause frequently.
9 Look at your audience.
10 Look interested.
11 Express yourself with your hands and face.
12 Don't dance; don't stand on one leg.
13 Refer to your notes as little as possible.
14 Don't cover your face.
15 Outline what you are going to say.
16 Summarise the main points.
17 Respect the time limit.

2 Widen your advice and construct a list of 'do's' and 'don't's' under the following headings:

- quantity of information
- structuring information
- timing
- repetition and emphasis
- examples
- visuals and handouts
- anticipating the needs of your audience
- establishing authority and credibility.

6.2.B
Presenting skills

Presenting a short talk

In small groups, present a short talk (maximum of ten minutes) based on the following study which you have carried out in advance.

The methodology is as follows:

1 Choose a brand from one of the following product families:

- cleaning products
- savoury snacks
- soft drinks
- DIY
- confectionery
- condiments
- soap and cosmetics
- rice and pasta.

2 Visit a local supermarket, hypermarket or large store where your product is sold.

3 Fill in the following information sheet.

4 Prepare and present your short talk.

Information sheet for Exercise 6.2.B

Name of store:
Size (m²):
Product (name of product plus short description):
Floor space for product family (m):
Total shelf space for product family (m):
Total shelf space for product (m):
Location within store:
Plan of shelves where product located:

5
4
3
2
1

Comments and observations:
Recommendations for improving sales of product:

6.2.C
Analysis

Retailing trends

In small groups, study Figures 13 to 17. Choose one point of interest, develop it and present it to the class in a short talk (maximum three minutes). Remember to give your talk a title and to respect the guidelines on page 78.

Figure 13:
Sales figures for the biggest retailers in the US, Britain, France, Italy, Germany and Spain (1991)

Country	Retailer	£ billion	Country	Retailer	£ billion
USA			**GB**		
1	Wall-Mart	18.7	1	Sainsbury	7.3
2	Kmart	18.4	2	Marks and Spencer	5.5
3	Sears Roebuck	18.3	3	Tesco	5.4
4	American Stores	12.7	4	Argyll	4.1
5	Kroger Co	11.6	5	Asda	3.5
6	JC Penney	9.4	6	Boots	3.4
7	Safeway	8.5	7	Kingfisher	2.9
8	Dayton Hudson	8.4	8	GUS	2.7
9	A + P	6.5	9	Sears	2.1
10	May	5.8	10	Kwik Save	1.5
France			**Italy**		
1	Leclerc	10.0	1	Coop Italia	3.5
2	Intermarché	9.6	2	Vege	1.9
3	Carrefour	7.6	3	La Rinascente	1.9
4	Promodès	5.8	4	Crai	1.7
5	Sucres et Denrées	4.7	5	Standa	1.7
6	Casino	4.5	6	Despar	1.6
7	Auchan	4.0	7	Cid	1.5
8	Cora	3.5	8	Conad	1.4
9	Pinault	3.3	9	A + O Selex	1.3
10	Système U	3.2	10	SME	1.2
Germany			**Spain**		
1	Metro	10.3	1	Pryca	1.6
2	Rewe	9.2	2	Continente	1.2
3	Aldi	8.1	3	Alcampo	1.0
4	Asko-Schaper-Coop	5.3	4	Mercadona	0.8
5	Kandstadt	5.3	5	Hiperco	0.5
6	Tengelmann	5.1			
7	Spar	4.3			
8	Hertie	2.3			
9	Lidl + Schwartz	2.0			
10	Allkauf	1.8			

Figure 14:
European market share for Europe's top 10 retailers (1991)

1	Carrefour	F S	4.2%
2	Aldi	G N D F GB	3.9%
3	Leclerc	F	3.8%
=	Intermarché	F	3.8%
=	Promodès	F S P G I	3.8%
6	Sainsbury	GB	2.9%
7	Rewe Leibrand	G	2.8%
8	Tengelmann	G	2.5%
9	Tesco	GB Ire	2.4%
10	Auchan	F S	2.3%

The following abbreviations have been used in this table:

F:	France	GB:	Great Britain
S:	Spain	G:	Germany
P:	Portugal	N:	Netherlands
I:	Italy	D:	Denmark
Ire:	Ireland	B:	Belgium

Figure 15:
Food retailers in the EC (1991)

Number of retail outlets: 514,000   Sales: £209 billion

GB 9.7% France 8.9% Former West Germany 13.4% 20.4% Italy 27.8% Spain 19.8%

Other countries
Portugal 8.3
Greece 5.0
Belgium 2.7
Netherlands 1.7
Ireland 1.7
Denmark 1.0

Other countries
Netherlands 4.5
Belgium 3.5
Denmark 2.5
Greece 1.8
Ireland 1.4
Portugal 1.0

GB 17.9% France 28.3% Italy 8.5% Spain 8.7% 21.9% 14.7% Former West Germany

Figure 16:
Hypermarket yield in £ per m2 for total European operations

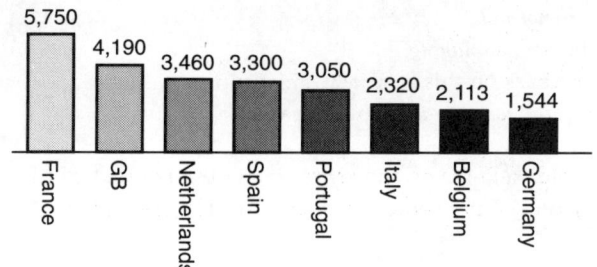

France	GB	Netherlands	Spain	Portugal	Italy	Belgium	Germany
5,750	4,190	3,460	3,300	3,050	2,320	2,113	1,544

Figure 17:
European market share for Europe's top 10 retailers

1987	25.0%
1988	26.8%
1989	31.4%

Retailing

6.3.A

Listening

Warehouse clubs

Listen to the tape recording of a marketer talking about warehouse clubs in America. Answer the following questions.

1 Supply the following figures:

    a The percentage discount offered by warehouse clubs compared with prices in other retail outlets.

    b The number of warehouse clubs in the USA.

    c Total expected sales this year.

    d Inventory turnover by successful warehouse clubs.

    e The cost of becoming a member of a warehouse club.

    f The club's gross margin.

    g The percentage of purchases made by business customers.

2 Identify six factors which enable warehouse clubs to offer such huge discounts.

3 What impact have warehouse clubs had on retailing generally, and why?

6.3.B

Vocabulary

Adjectives

I In each of the following sentences replace the words in italics with a more complex adjective from the list below.

colossal	fierce	slack	slender	burning
conventional	reckless	first rate	critical	lax
destructive	gratifying	handy		

1 Bicorex plc is facing *very hard* competition.
2 Sales were *very slow* last year.
3 A *very important* decision was made.
4 He made a *very big* mistake.
5 This product only has a *very small* chance of succeeding.
6 My job is *very nice*.
7 She is a *very good* salesperson.
8 He had a *very strong* desire to buy a sports car.
9 It's *very convenient* to shop at the local supermarket.
10 Our sales approach is *very normal*.
11 A new price war could be *very damaging*.
12 I refuse to allow you to embark on this *extremely risky* venture.
13 Our salespeople have become *too casual* about their work.

2 What images do the complex adjectives convey to you in the context of the above sentences? Portray one of the sentences pictorially for use with an overhead projector.

6.3.C
Grammar

Word transformation

1 Complete the following *sentences by* transforming the words in italics.

Example

> Profits have been affected by wide *fluctuate* in the market over the past
> year → fluctuations

1 Our chain of *distribute* is too long; we ought to cut out the middleman.
2 A *short* of top marketing executives has made recruitment pretty difficult.
3 Yuppies tend to find this product rather *appeal*.
4 Government *regulate* require all ingredients to be clearly displayed on the label.
5 The *grow* of hypermarkets has led to an increasing *concentrate* of powerful retailers.
6 We simply can't *competition* with them on price.
7 Our *sell* figures are down by 3.5%.
8 We'll have to make some *alter* if the campaign is to succeed.
9 The Japanese simply *production* better quality goods.
10 We've made a *size* increase in our market share.
11 New patterns of *consume* have evolved over the past few years.
12 The *sell* are always polite and helpful.
13 We're expecting a slight *reduce* in orders next month.
14 *Consume* are *increase* fed up with being given misleading information.
15 This *advertise* will be broadcast on all the *commerce* television networks in the Fall.
16 People's net *dispose* income has steadily risen since the war.
17 We've made several interesting scientific *discover* but have been unable to transform them into *market* products.
18 It would be much more *economy* to buy them in bulk.
19 Our next step is to *conquest* the Australian market.
20 We need to *diverse* our product range.

2 Write a short paragraph using five of the untransformed words in italics.

6.3.D
Listening

A shopping mall

Listen to the tape recording of a talk about a large shopping mall in Los Angeles and answer these questions.

1 What five changes in post-war American society led to the creation of the first shopping malls?
2 What did Victor Gruen hope that the shopping mall would achieve?
3 What facilities can be found at this LA mall?
4 How does the layout of the mall encourage customers to spend more money than planned?
5 Apart from being convenient and offering a wide range of products and amenities, what other advantages does this mall offer?
6 In what way can this mall be considered a fantasy land?

Discussion

The future of retailing

In small groups, discuss the changes which you foresee in retailing in your country over the next 20 years.

Use the following points to guide your discussion:

- the decline/disapearance of some retail outlets
- the appearance/growth of other retail outlets
- changes in location of retail outlets
- changes in consumption patterns (frequency of shopping, growth of new products, etc)
- government regulations and deregulations
- demographic trends, economic growth, development of infrastructure and so on.

COMPANY FOCUS
Marketing at United Distillers

The following extracts are taken from Guinness plc's annual report for 1991. Read them and then answer the questions which follow.

UNITED DISTILLERS

United Distillers, the spirits company of Guinness PLC, produces and markets premium quality, world-famous brands. It is the international leader in both the Scotch whisky and gin industries, and is the world's largest and most profitable spirits company.

The company employs nearly 11,000 people worldwide. It has a portfolio of leading brands of Scotch whisky, gin, bourbon, vodka, rum and other spirits. More than 50 million cases are sold annually.

United Distillers' international sales and marketing headquarters is at Landmark House, Hammersmith, London. Distillers House, Ellersly Road, Edinburgh, is the headquarters for UK production. United Distillers has four geographical regions: Europe, North America, Asia/Pacific and International (rest of the world), with an Operations Group responsible for UK production.

In overseas markets the company owns sales and marketing companies, has joint ventures, notably with LVMH (Moët Hennessy Louis Vuitton), and has direct control over 80% of its brands distribution. It also produces spirits locally, either directly or through third party arrangements.

PERFORMANCE

The Top Five Wines & Spirits Companies in the World
(Operating Profit – 1991)

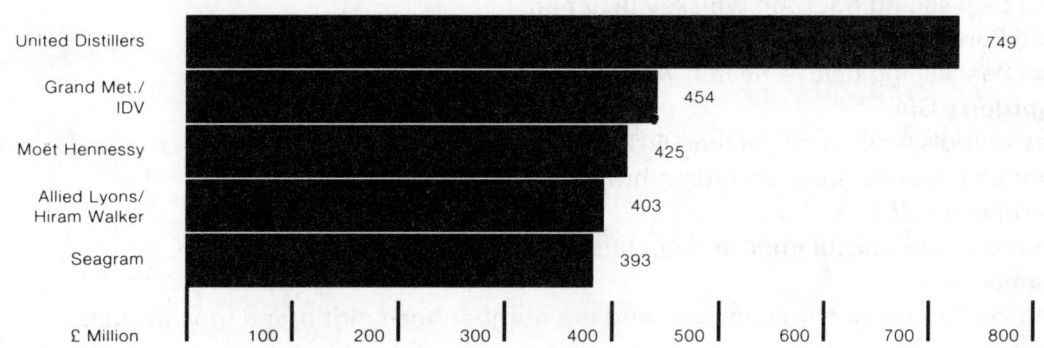

Source: International Drinks Bulletin

NB: Figures are adjusted for recent acquisitions to reflect a full year basis

UNITED DISTILLERS' PRINCIPAL BRANDS – 1991

World Spirits Ranking	Brand	1991 Volume in millions of nine litre cases
4	Johnnie Walker Red Label	6.6
5	Gordon's Gin	6.4
15	Bell's	4.0
28	Dewar's White Label	3.0
29	Johnnie Walker Black Label	2.9
39	Gordon's Vodka	2.4
54	Pampero Rum	2.0
58	White Horse Fine Old	1.9
81	Tanqueray Gin	1.4
86	Skol (vodka)	1.3
91	Asbach Uralt (German brandy)	1.3

Source: Impact International January 1992 (Volumes measured are **shipments** not customer sales.)

KEY BRANDS

United Distillers' comprehensive portfolio includes internationally famous brand names such as:-

Johnnie Walker Red Label
the world's best selling Scotch and the leading duty free spirits brand worldwide.

Johnnie Walker Black Label
the world's best selling deluxe Scotch whisky, and the world's third largest duty free spirits brand.

Bell's Extra Special
the best selling Scotch whisky in the UK and South Africa.

Dewar's White Label
the best selling Scotch whisky in the USA, and the fifth largest Scotch brand in the world.

White Horse Fine Old
the best selling Scotch whisky in Japan, and the seventh largest Scotch brand in the world.

I W Harper
the best selling bourbon whiskey in Japan.

Old Parr
the best selling deluxe Scotch whisky in Japan.

Gordon's Gin
the world's leading gin, selling 50% more volume than its nearest gin competitor, and United Distillers' largest volume brand.

Tanqueray Gin
the most successful imported gin in the USA.

Pampero Rum
the world's leading golden rum, and the number one spirit brand in Venezuela.

Asbach Uralt
the leading premium brandy in Germany.

Bundaberg Rum
the biggest spirits brand in Australia.

United Distillers is the largest company in the Scotch whisky industry and during 1991 continued to strengthen this position with the rejuvenation and range development of key brands.

Johnnie Walker, the world's best selling Scotch whisky, is United Distillers' flagship brand.

The Company has now established a broad range of Johnnie Walker products, at carefully selected positioning and price points. Red Label is the brand's premium standard Scotch. Black Label its 12-year-old de luxe, while Swing is positioned at the top end of the de luxe sector. Following a successful launch into duty free. Premier was introduced into Asia Pacific domestic markets during 1991 at XO cognac price level, and the top of the range is Johnnie Walker Blue Label, selling at over $100 in prestige outlets only.

To reinforce the brand's unique role in golf sponsorship, the inaugural Johnnie Walker World Championship was held in Jamaica. This annual event, which is the play-off between the winners of the season's leading tournaments, generated considerable worldwide interest and is to be held again in Jamaica in December 1992.

Old Parr has been the leading de luxe Scotch whisky in Japan for many years, with considerable sales in Latin America too. The brand takes its name from the legendary figure of Thomas Parr who, it was claimed, lived to the age of 152, through the reigns of 10 monarchs from 1483–1635.

Old Parr's premium range extension. Old Parr Superior, continues to build sales steadily in both Japan and duty free. Old Parr Tribute, presented in a ceramic bottle, took the brand into the premium duty free gift market. Old Parr Elizabethan, only available in duty free, is the flagship of the range, selling at over $700,

enhancing the prestigious image of the Old Parr brand and of Scotch whisky overall.

White Horse is another of the world's top selling Scotch whiskies. It is the premium brand leader in Japan as well as having a strong customer franchise in the UK, South America and continental Europe.

During the year, the brand has undergone a major repackaging following extensive research in its key markets. This has led to the introduction of a more distinctive bottle which reflects the quality the consumer expects of this brand. In Japan, a new bottle with an 8-year-old blend has been introduced for that market alone.

White Horse also has an extended range in the Japanese market, where White Horse Extra Fine, positioned between the standard and de luxe categories, has shown good growth. Additionally, Glen Elgin, a single malt, was launched under the White Horse brand name. Its launch reflects the increasing interest in malts in Japan.

United Distillers continued to develop its other single malt brands. The Classic Malts – six premium-priced malts representing the different whisky-producing regions of Scotland – have extended their distribution from duty free to major European markets and the USA Cardhu's packaging was upgraded to enhance its unique positioning.

Locally-bottled Scotch also fulfils an important role in extending United Distiller's coverage of the overall Scotch whisky market. The launch of Usher's Green Stripe was an outstanding success in Venezuela in providing an opportunity to trade up from national whiskies. Scoresby, recently acquired as part of the Glenmore portfolio and locally bottled in the USA, is now the fourth largest Scotch whisky in that market.

---

1 How has United Distillers segmented its markets both geographically and in terms of quality and image?

2 What role does Old Parr Elizabethan play in the Old Parr product range?

3 How much importance does United Distillers attach to packaging?

4 Why do you think Glen Elgin was launched under the White Horse brand name?

5 In which way is United Distillers much more than a producer of spirits?

6 What is meant by a 'flagship brand'?

7 From what you have read in the above extracts and from your background knowledge, describe the ways in which United Distillers have achieved a coherent and successful Marketing Mix.

PART III
Finance

UNIT 7
Raising capital

The sources of funds

7.I.A

7.I.A
Warm-up

National projects

In small groups discuss the following questions:

1 What large projects are currently being carried out or have recently been carried out in your country?

2 How are these projects being financed?

3 Do you know of any small projects and if so, how are these being financed?

7.I.B
Reading

Raising capital

Read the following passage and answer the questions which follow it.

In order to meet the day-to-day expenses of running a business and to acquire new assets, companies need to raise funds. Financing day-to-day operations such as buying inventory or paying wages are very different from financing a project that may only bear fruit in five years time. Consequently, financial matters are often discussed in terms of different time periods.

Short-term finance
A company's revenues don't always come in at exactly the same rate as the bills which have to be paid. To avoid having a negative cash flow the company may need to take on some short-term debt which would be repaid within one year. The main sources of short-term financing are as follows: trade credit is obtained by the purchaser directly from the supplier and in most countries is the most widespread source of short-term financing for business. The terms of the trade credit vary according to the amount of credit required and the company's credit rating. Some suppliers may offer their customers 30 days or 60 days of interest-free credit on a handshake. This is known as open-book credit. Hire purchase is another kind of trade credit. In This case the customer takes possession of the goods immediately in return for a deposit plus regular instalments.

Other suppliers prefer a written agreement, called a promissory note, whereby the customer (who initiates it) promises to repay a fixed sum of money plus interest on a specified date in return for immediate credit.

Another type of trade credit is a trade draft which is similar to the promissory note except that it is drawn up by the supplier and not the customer. Trade drafts are particularly useful when dealing with foreign customers whose credit ratings are difficult to check.

Short-term loans may be obtained from a commercial bank or a finance company which charges interest depending on the borrower's creditworthiness. A secured loan is a loan backed by collateral, which is an asset such as property, inventory or accounts receivable (amounts owed by customers). If the borrower fails to repay the loan, the lender may seize the asset.

Businesses may also be able to sell accounts receivable to a financial institution. This is known as factoring and tends to be a relatively expensive way of raising short-term capital.

An unsecured loan requires no collateral. However, the lender may require the borrower to maintain a minimum amount of money at the bank while the loan is outstanding. This is known as a compensating balance. Although the borrower pays interest on the full amount of the loan, a portion of it remains on deposit at the bank. Another important type of unsecured loan is an overdraft, or line of credit, whereby the business may borrow an agreed-on maximum amount of money without having to negotiate each time with the bank.

Commercial paper is a financing option which is mainly for large corporations with top credit ratings. In order to finance short-term projects a corporation may sell commercial paper to another business which will pay less than its face value. At the end of the stipulated period the corporation will buy back the commercial paper at full face value, the difference between the discounted price and the face value being the equivalent of interest on a loan.

Long-term finance

In order to finance long-term projects such as major construction, acquisition of other companies, and R & D projects, companies can turn to both internal and external sources of capital. The chief internal source is retained earnings which is the money kept by the firm after meeting its expenses and distributing a portion of the profits to investors. Retained earnings are also known as ploughed-back profits or reserves. Another source of capital is to sell assets such as real estate.

External sources of capital may be divided into two broad categories: debt capital (which must be repaid) and equity capital (which represents investors' shares of ownership in the company). There are three kinds of debt capital:

Long-term loans are repaid over a period of five years or more and may be either secured or unsecured. Collateral on a secured loan is usually in the form of a mortgage.

Leasing is a source of long-term capital whereby a company borrows an item (a machine, a building, a vehicle) in exchange for regular payments. The leasing arrangement often includes an option to buy.

Bonds are transferable certificates that pay interest regularly for the term of the loan and may be either secured or unsecured. Unsecured bonds are called debentures.

As far as equity capital is concerned, the source of equity for a small company is often a single individual such as a member of the family or a venture capitalist. In partnerships, a new partner may be brought in thus providing a fresh source of equity. In larger businesses equity may be raised though the Stock Exchange where shares are issued to investors on the open market. In each case the investor owns a share in the business and expects a share in the profits.

1 What is the difference between:

    a debt capital and equity capital?
    b leasing and hire purchase?
    c secured bonds and debentures?
    d interest and dividends?
    e open-book credit and promissory notes?

7.1.C
Presenting

Using overheads

In making oral presentations it is essential to convey important information visually, using slides or an overhead projector wherever possible. The keys to successful visuals are *simplicity* and *clarity*. It also helps if your visuals are *eye-catching*.

Imagine you have been asked to present an outline of the text on page 90 to a group of trainee managers. Draw up a chart which could be used on an overhead projector to convey the main points of the text visually.

7.1.D
Vocabulary

Defining key terms

1 Match the following key terms with their definitions:

Terms	Definitions
1 asset	**a** a loan agreement whereby the lender has a legal claim on the borrower's property if repayments are not made as specified
2 inventory	
3 cash flow	**b** payments to shareholders from a company's earnings
4 credit rating	**c** the degree of risk a borrower represents
5 trade credit	**d** valuable things owned by a company
6 open book credit	**e** payment terms whereby the purchaser takes possession of the goods and pays for them later
7 promissory note	**f** payment terms whereby the purchaser takes possession of the goods upon payment of a deposit and regular instalments
8 trade draft	**g** a company's promise to pay back a stated amount of money on a given date less than one year from the time of issue
9 secured loan	
10 hire purchase	**h** an order to pay a stated amount of money within a certain number of days, drawn up by the creditor
11 collateral	
12 factoring	**i** an unconditional written promise to repay a certain sum of money on a specified date, drawn up by the customer
13 unsecured loan	
	j money owed by customers
14 compensating balance	**k** a legal agreement whereby the user of an asset pays the owner in exchange for using the asset
15 line of credit/ overdraft	**l** bonds that are not backed by specific assets
	m a market where stocks and bonds are traded
16 accounts receivable	**n** bonds that pay a high interest rate because of the low credit rating of the borrower
17 commercial paper	**o** a loan granted on the basis of the borrower's credit rating rather than on the basis of collateral
18 retained earnings	**p** a tangible asset that a lender can claim if a borrower defaults on a loan
	q the net increase in assets which can be ploughed back into the business
19 mortgage	**r** goods held in stock for the production process or for sale to final customers
20 lease	**s** a loan backed up with something of value that the lender can claim in case of default
21 bond	**t** the portion of an unsecured loan that is kept on deposit at the bank
22 debentures	**u** the amount of money entering and leaving a business
23 junk bonds	**v** an unsecured short-term loan made available up to a certain amount
24 dividends	**w** funds obtained by selling shares of ownership in the company
25 equity	**x** a certificate of indebtedness sold to raise funds
26 Stock Exchange	**y** credit obtained by the purchaser directly from the supplier
	z the buying of accounts receivable at a discount

2 Divide into two teams. Each member of each team reads aloud a definition and asks one member of the opposing team to give the corresponding term. The person answering must not consult his or her notes and has five seconds to answer in order to earn a point.

Sources of funds: pros and cons

Discussion

From what you have read in exercise 7.1.B and from your background knowledge list the possible advantages and disadvantages of raising funds through the following sources:

1 open-book credit	6 commercial paper
2 promissory notes	7 long-term loans
3 trade drafts	8 leasing
4 secured loans	9 bonds
5 unsecured loans	10 equity

7.1.F

Role play

Giving and getting information

Work in pairs sitting back-to-back. One of you plays Role A and the other Role B.

Role A

You have just received your monthly bank statement as shown in Figure 18. Unfortunately, it was poorly printed and some important information is missing. Phone your bank and ask them to give you the missing information.

Figure 18:
Monthly bank statement for Role A

EASTERN BANK
Westbourne

Mr JAMES PEACH
13 Orchard Ave
WESTCLIFF, DORSET

Tel. 0202 778925

STATEMENT OF ACCOUNT
A/C No 906243077
31. JAN 93
Post No 14

DETAILS	PAYMENTS	RECEIPTS	DATE	BALANCE
Balance forward			31.12	1 460.00
Cash withdrawal	1 300.00		2.1	160.00
Nego. of us chq		47.25	2.1	207.25
Card: happy eater	27.50		5.1	179.75
Card: wine and dine	31.25		6.1	148.50
Salary credit		1 745.25	15.1	1 893.75
STO: elect	102.00		18.1	1 791.75
STO: mortgage	₃.00		18.1	75
DDR: northern assurance	0.00		18.1	+05.75
Cheque 373214	₂₅		2.1	₃₂₃.50
Cheque 373215	₃2.50		5.1	₃.00
Cheque 373218	415.00		20.1	−118.00
Cheque 373221	372.50		22.1	−490.50
Dr				−490.50
Bank charges	18.00		31.1	
DR			31.1	−508.50

Abbreviations: DIV Dividend ; STO Standing Order ; DDR Direct Debit ; DR Overdrawn Balance ; CDT Cash Dispenser Transaction ; BGC Bank Giro Credit

You paid in a cheque last week for £450 but this does not appear on the statement. Ask the bank why not. You also want an explanation for the high bank charges and say that generally you are unsatisfied with the bank's service.

Role B

You are a teller at Eastern Bank. You receive a phone call from a customer. Obtain his references, then call up his account on your screen (Figure 19) and give him the information he requires.

Figure 19:
Monthly bank statement for Role B

EASTERN BANK
Westbourne   Tel. 0202 778925

Mr JAMES PEACH   STATEMENT OF ACCOUNT
13 Orchard Ave   A/C No 906243077
WESTCLIFF, DORSET   31. JAN 93
                                                               Post No 14

DETAILS	PAYMENTS	RECEIPTS	DATE	BALANCE
Balance forward			31.12	1 460.00
Cash withdrawal	1 300.00		2.1	160.00
Nego. of us chq		47.25	2.1	207.25
Card: happy eater	27.50		5.1	179.75
Card: wine and dine	31.25		6.1	148.50
Salary credit		1 745.25	15.1	1 893.75
STO: elect	102.00		18.1	1 791.75
STO: mortgage	876.00		18.1	1 75.75
DDR: northern assurance	300.00		18.1	1 405.75
Cheque 373214	76.25		2.1	1 329.50
Cheque 373215	1 032.50		5.1	297.00
Cheque 373218	415.00		20.1	−118.00
Cheque 373221	372.50		22.1	−490.50
Dr			−490.50	
Bank charges	18.00		31.1	
DR			31.1	−508.50

Abbreviations: DIV Dividend ; STO Standing Order ; DDR Direct Debit ; DR Overdrawn Balance ; CDT Cash Dispenser Transaction ; BGC Bank Giro Credit

After investigation, you find a cheque for £450 was credited to the customer's account this morning. The delay was caused by the regional computer being out of order for 48 hours. The bank charges are for the unauthorised overdraft incurred during the month (£10.00) and the US dollar cheque (£8.00). You offer to make the customer an appointment to see the manager to discuss the service offered by the bank.

Section 2

The uses of funds

7.2.A

Discussion

Meeting the company's needs

In small groups, discuss what you think would be the likely source or sources of funds in the following cases. Make a copy of the grid and fill it in accordingly. Be ready to justify your decisions.

Company	Needs	Source(s) of funds
1 Computer manufacturer (annual earnings 1992: $3 billion)	to buy new plant and equipment	
2 Medium-sized car dealer	to buy 12 vehicles for immediate display in showroom (prime lending rate: 13%)	
3 Small producer of kitchen furniture	to have enough ready cash to cover immediate expenses	
4 Small manufacturer	to purchase 10 industrial drills	
5 Large producer of ski-ing equipment with top credit-rating	to meet immediate expenses during off-season (prime lending rate: 18%)	
6 Overseas electronics wholesaler with unknown credit rating	to buy a large consignment of VCRs	
7 Clothes store with poor credit rating	to purchase stock for the summer season	
8 Major oil company	to build a 1,000 km pipeline from a newly discovered oil-field to the sea	
9 Leading chemical manufacturer	to finance acquisition of a major competitor (forecast: two or three years before business takes off again)	

Getting the message across

In writing reports and memos, and in presenting information orally, we are often called upon to state or restate the main facts and arguments as briefly as possible.

Match each of the following long sentences with a short sentence.

Long sentences

1 It is probably quite true to say that to a certain extent the borrower's choice of options in financing a project depends in many cases on the probable cost of the project.

2 Raising funds through the sale of certificates of indebtedness is less onerous, financially speaking, than other ways of raising capital.

3 Individuals and institutions owning bonds in a particular company are not allowed to interfere in the way it runs its business.

4 There are many arguments for and against the decision by a company to obtain fresh capital through the sale of shares on the Stock Exchange.

5 Raising capital through borrowing from banks, individuals, companies or any other institution can turn out to be a costly operation at times when rates of interest tend to be high.

Short sentences

a The Stock Exchange cannot meet the needs of all companies.

b When interest rates are high, any form of debt is expensive.

c It is relatively easy to issue bonds.

d Bondholders do not have any voice in management.

e Bonds represent the cheapest type of financing.

f Choosing a vehicle for financing a project often depends on the size of the operation.

g Issuing stock has its pros and cons.

h The choice of project a company undertakes depends on the capital it is able to raise.

i Buying shares can be expensive.

Why are the short sentences better models to follow than the long sentences?

Simplifying and reducing

A good summary should:
● be objective – your comments or opinions should not be included
● be in your own words
● include only essential material
● be concise – it should be no longer than one-third of the original work and may be as short as one sentence.

Rewrite each of the following sentences, preserving the essential meaning, in a maximum of one-third of the original number of words.

1 It is undeniably the case that the growing number of consumers who purchase goods and services using any one of a number of credit cards has led to a situation where banks are reaping huge profits. (36 words)

2 It is most regrettable that there is clear evidence which indicates that certain consumers in our society are purchasing more than they can afford due to credit cards. (28 words)

3 It would appear reasonable to assert that more stringent measures need to be set up and put into practice by the banks themselves if we are not to witness the tragedy of growing numbers of families being forced into a situation of living in a state of permanent indebtedness. (49 words)

4 It really was totally and utterly irresponsible of loan managers from banks throughout the United States as well as Western Europe and Japan to have acted in such a way as to extend large-scale credit facilities to undeveloped and developing countries whose economies simply have not been able to support the enormous burden of interest repayments. (57 words)

7.2.D
Vocabulary

Verbs and nouns in context

I Match the phrases on the left with those on the right to make complete sentences.

1 We should be able to *meet* ...	a on the loan.
2 We'll need to *raise* ...	b our accounts receivable.
3 If we don't use our reserves, we'll simply have to *take on* ...	c all the profits.
	d our expenses this year.
4 If you buy on hire purchase, you have to *put down* ...	e a deposit.
5 It may be more expensive to *pay by* ...	f funds for the expansion programme.
6 We'll ask our supplier to *draw up* ...	g a trade draft.
7 It will work out very expensive to *factor* ...	h instalments.
8 Let's *lease* ...	i all the vehicles.
9 I hope they don't *default* ...	j more debt.
10 Instead of giving a dividend this year, why don't we *plough back* ...	

2 Find the nouns which correspond to the following verbs.

Example

> To indicate → indication

1	to repay	13	to seize
2	to extend	14	to require
3	to purchase	15	to negotiate
4	to reap	16	to sell
5	to acquire	17	to distribute
6	to discuss	18	to divide
7	to avoid	19	to lease
8	to vary	20	to own
9	to agree	21	to expect
10	to promise	22	to specify
11	to back	23	to earn
12	to fail	24	to rate

3 Fill in the blanks in the following paragraph, using nouns from the previous exercise, so that it respects the meaning of the paragraph which follows.

'The _____ 1 _____ of the government to provide sufficient _____ 2 _____ for the project has led to a _____ 3 _____ among the members of the Board of Directors. Some want to reopen _____ 4* _____ with the government in the hope of obtaining more cash, while others feel we should ask the banks for a(n) _____ 5 _____ of the _____ 6 _____ of the loan. My main worry is that if neither plan works, we'll have to consider the _____ 7 _____ of our American operations which will lead to a major loss of _____ 8 _____ . Hopefully, though, we'll come to some kind of a(n) _____ 9 _____ before long.

*two possibilities

'The government has not funded the project sufficiently and the Board is now split over whether to try again or ask the banks to restructure the debt. I'm concerned that if we don't come up with a solution, we may have to discontinue our business in the States, with the resulting drop in income. Let's hope we can sort something out soon!'

7.2.E

Discussion

Sayings

Each language has 'sayings' about money. Discuss the ideas behind the English sayings shown below. Translate similar sayings about money from other languages you know and compare the advice they offer.

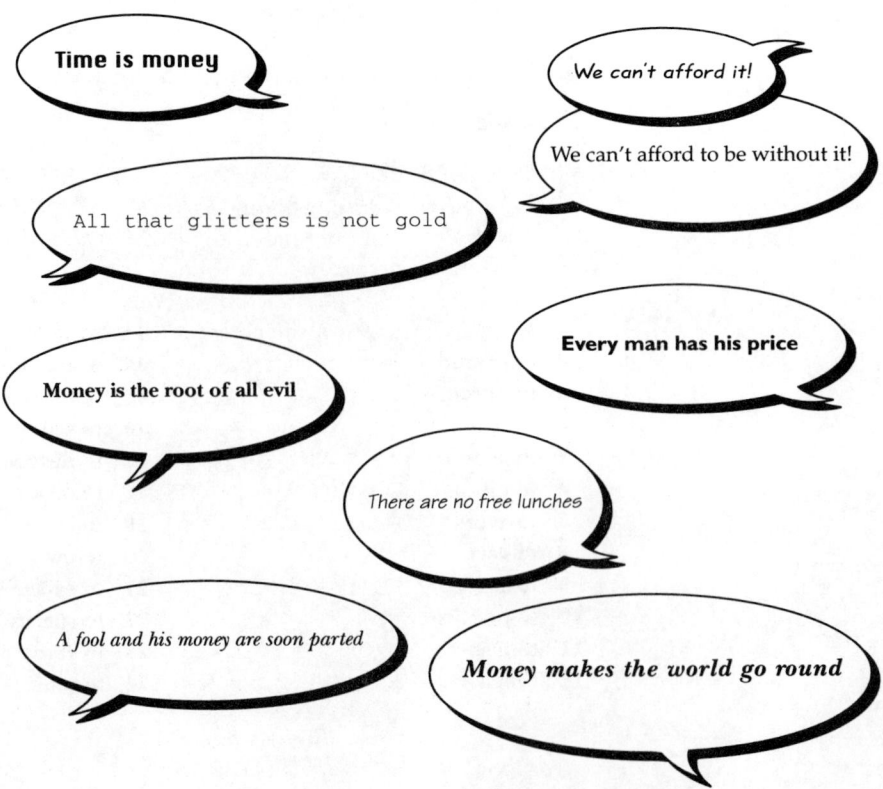

UNIT 8
Investing

Investment options

Investment options

Read the following article from *'Investment Quarterly'* then work on exercises 8.1.B and 8.1.C.

Purchasing plant, machinery, management contracts, patents, and other real assets is necessary if companies are to grow and remain competitive. Investment decisions such as these are based on the need to find assets which are worth more than they cost and which are worth more than other investments. Calculating how much a real asset is worth is often a difficult task. Unlike securities investments which are traded in highly active markets, the market for most corporate investments is relatively thin; for example, it is not often that one comes across advertisements in The Financial Times to sell an oil refinery, buy a second-hand blast furnace, or exchange a patent.

Financial managers are therefore called upon to analyse mountains of raw data supplied by armies of specialists in product design, production, marketing and so on, in order to make forecasts upon which their investment decisions will be based.

But even where a flourishing market does exist, the choice of investment is not easy as the number of investment products on the market has increased dramatically over the past few years. Before investing your money you need to analyse your resources and objectives. Determining what you are looking for in terms of income, growth, safety, liquidity and tax benefits will help you develop an efficient investment strategy.

If you are looking for a steady income from your investment the best strategy would be to choose low-risk vehicles – bank deposits, Government securities, high-grade corporate bonds and stock – which pay interest or dividends on a regular basis.

If, however, you are more interested in growth you may be better off choosing an investment which maximises the potential for capital gains. Stocks, real estate, precious metals or works of art may be the answer, although this depends very much on the prevailing economic conditions.

In general, the higher the potential for income or growth, the greater the risk of the investment. For example, the rate of return on junk bonds tends to be high, but so are the risks.

If liquidity is important to you – in other words, if you may need to convert the investment into cash soon – you should invest in something the price of which does not fluctuate too much. If not, you may have to sell when the market is down.

Stocks

Stocks can earn money in two ways: by paying dividends and through capital gains. Blue chip stocks are issued by large, well-capitalised companies that have consistently paid good dividends. On the other hand, stocks which offer high capital gains are more difficult to identify. The likelihood of a particular stock increasing in market value depends on a variety of factors, not least of which is the condition of the market as a whole. Stock prices tend to rise and fall as the economy expands and contracts. A 'bear' market is characterised by falling share values and generally occurs during recessions. A 'bull' market, on the other hand, is associated with economic booms and is characterised by rising share prices.

Corporate bonds

Corporate bonds offer income in the form of interest plus the possibility of making capital gains. Although corporate bonds are relatively safe investments, their face value can fluctuate, and may go down as well as up, thereby leading to a capital loss. However, this may not matter much to investors whose objective is to receive regular interest; the capital loss only occurs when the bond is sold and such investors may have no intention of selling.

Government securities

Federal and state governments also issue bonds which, generally speaking, carry a lower rate of interest than corporate bonds but provide advantages in terms of safety and tax advantages. In the US, the main government securities are as follows:

- Treasury bills (T-bills) are sold by the US government at a discount and redeemed at full face value at maturity, which ranges from 91 to 364 days from the date of issue. A minimum investment of $10,000 is required.
- Treasury notes and bonds have longer maturity dates than T-bills and pay a fixed rate of tax-free interest twice a year, which is generally about one percentage point less than the interest on corporate bonds. A minimum investment of $1,000 is required.
- Savings bonds are available in denominations ranging from $50 to $10,000. Although savings bonds can be sold at any time, the interest rate is higher if the holder keeps them for at least five years.
- Municipal bonds are tax-free investments issued by a town or city to help finance new public services. Many investors have become dissatisfied with municipal bonds, especially since a number of issuers defaulted on the repayments. ·

Mutual funds

A mutual fund is an investment company where small investors pool their money. This money is then used to acquire stocks or bonds or other financial investments. Small investors who have neither the time nor the know-how to invest rationally can benefit from the broad selection of investments which the fund is able to acquire. Mutual funds generally offer liquidity. They also offer variety and, in many cases, are tailored to specific objectives, for example, tax-exempt funds, high-growth funds, utility funds, money market funds and so on.

Commodities

Commodities are raw materials and farm produce used to produce finished goods. Producers and manufacturers need to hedge their risks and therefore follow very closely the fluctuations in the prices of the raw materials they produce or use. Contracts calling for the delivery at a given time of a set amount of these commodities are traded at Commodity Exchanges. The trade represents a shift in risk from the hedger to the speculator. Nowadays, many commodity traders are neither producers nor consumers but merely investors who will never take possession of the commodity. The commodity market is divided into 'spot trading' (for commodities that will be delivered immediately) and 'futures trading' (for commodities that will be delivered at a future date).

Financial futures

Investors in financial futures trade contracts for the delivery or acceptance of some financial instrument on a set date at a set price. Examples of financial instruments are Government securities, foreign currencies, loans, stock index futures and stock index options. Most financial futures are traded on 'the margin', a particular kind of leverage which means that the investor borrows from the broker, paying interest on the borrowed money and leaving the security with the broker as collateral.

8.1.B
Vocabulary

Defining key terms

Match the following terms with their definitions.

Terms
1 institutional investors
2 capital gains
3 speculators
4 rate of return
5 blue chip stocks
6 bull markets
7 bear markets
8 mutual fund
9 commodities
10 spot trading
11 futures trading
12 financial futures
13 hedgers
14 leverage
15 to default

Definitions
a Promises to buy or sell financial instruments at a future date.
b Companies that invest money entrusted to them by others.
c Trading in commodities that will be delivered at a future date.
d Raw materials used in producing other goods.
e Difference between the price at which a financial asset is sold and its original cost (assuming the price has gone up).
f Percentage increase in the value of an investment.
g Falling stock markets.
h Investors who seek large capital gains through relatively risky investment.
i Company that sells shares to the public and uses the pooled money to buy stocks, bonds, or other financial investments.
j Equity instruments issued by large, well-established companies and paying relatively stable dividends.
k Rising stock markets.
l Trading in commodities that will be delivered immediately.
m People who protect themselves from major fluctuations in prices which may lead to loss.
n The use of borrowed funds to finance a portion of an investment.
o Failure to pay back a debt.

8.1.C
Discussion

Where to invest

1 From your background knowledge, find examples of:
  ● institutional investors
  ● commodities
  ● blue-chip stocks
  ● real estate.

2 We are sorry to inform you that your Uncle Tom has passed away at the age of 103. You will, however, be pleased to know that he has left you $20,000 in his will. You have no immediate needs so you have decided to invest the money.

Explain to the class how you will invest the money. Justify your choice(s).

3 You are an investment consultant. Advise the following people on the best investment option(s).

Name	Age	Marital status	Profession	Size of investment	Other information
John McGregor	25	Single	Student	$12,000	Hopes to get married in two years' time
Anne Davies	59	Widow, no children	Secretary	$25,000	Receives a small widow's pension
James Black	37	Married, two children	Engineer	$100,000	Owns some real estate and wants to diversify
Marilyn Dangerfield	45	Married, children grown up	None	$150,000	Hopes to retire to Miami when she can afford to
Martha Leclerc	52	Married, four children	Owner and managing director of a company producing saucepans	$500,000	Worried about the effects that a rise in copper prices will have on her business

8.1.D

Role play

Consulting

Work in pairs. One student will play the role of investment consultant, while the other is the client. Prepare and present a short role play in which the consultant obtains information about the client's background, resources and needs and then advises him or her on the most appropriate investment.

The following expressions may be useful:

- What can I do for you?
- What size investment were you thinking of?
- How much risk are you prepared to take on?
- I'm looking for a high-yield investment.
- I want access to my capital at short notice.
- I want to put some money by for my daughter's university education.

8.1.E

Project

Analysing the stock market

In small groups, carry out the following analysis activities.

1 Choose an industry such as banking, electronics, food, manufacturing and so on. Select five companies within that industry the stock prices of which are listed in the *The New York Times* or *The Financial Times.*

2 Read the financial section of a good newspaper over one week and keep any articles regarding your chosen industry and companies.

3 Track the daily performance of your chosen companies over one week, using the guidelines below.

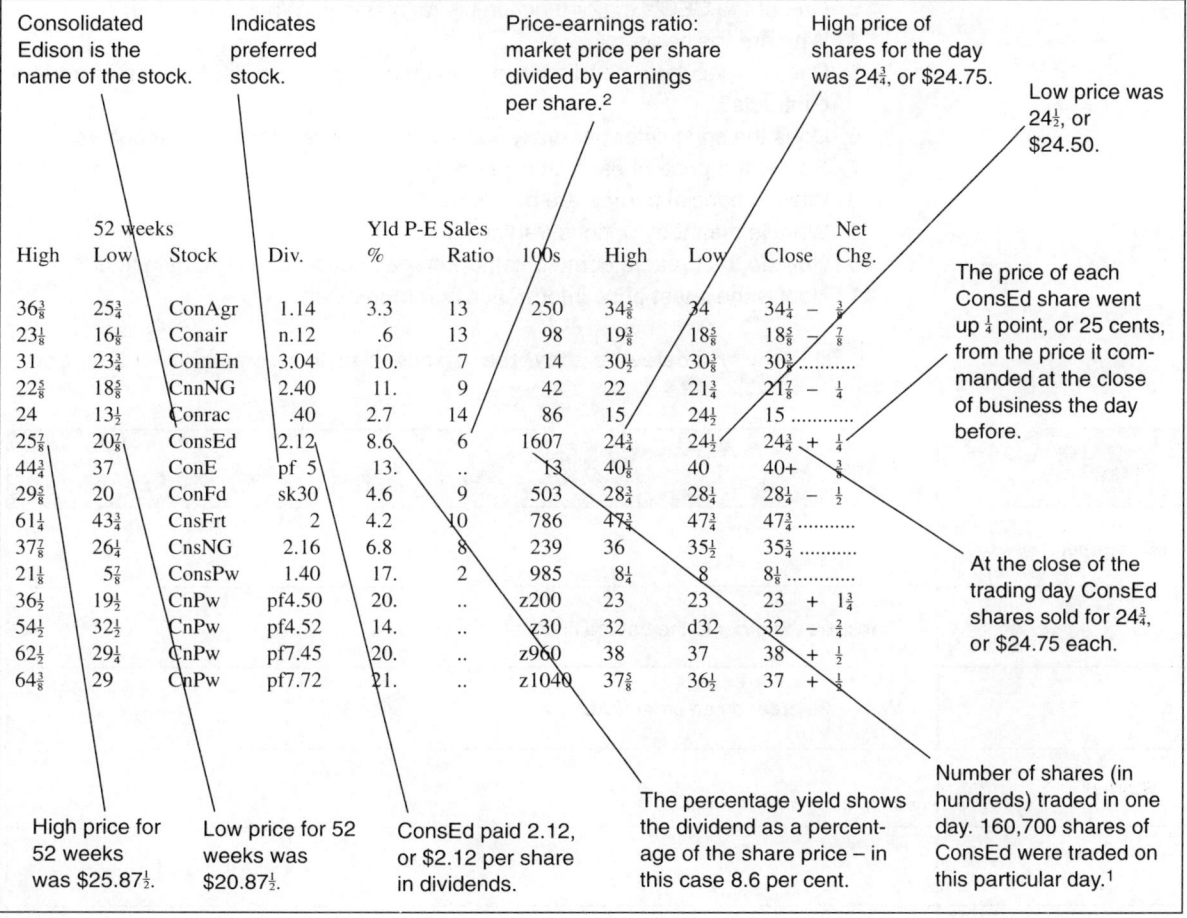

Consolidated Edison is the name of the stock.

Indicates preferred stock.

Price-earnings ratio: market price per share divided by earnings per share.[2]

High price of shares for the day was $24\frac{3}{4}$, or \$24.75.

Low price was $24\frac{1}{2}$, or \$24.50.

52 weeks High	52 weeks Low	Stock	Div.	Yld %	P-E Ratio	Sales 100s	High	Low	Close	Net Chg.
$36\frac{3}{8}$	$25\frac{3}{4}$	ConAgr	1.14	3.3	13	250	$34\frac{5}{8}$	34	$34\frac{1}{4}$	$-\frac{3}{8}$
$23\frac{1}{8}$	$16\frac{1}{8}$	Conair	n.12	.6	13	98	$19\frac{3}{8}$	$18\frac{5}{8}$	$18\frac{5}{8}$	$-\frac{7}{8}$
31	$23\frac{3}{4}$	ConnEn	3.04	10.	7	14	$30\frac{1}{2}$	$30\frac{3}{8}$	$30\frac{3}{8}$	....
$22\frac{5}{8}$	$18\frac{5}{8}$	CnnNG	2.40	11.	9	42	22	$21\frac{3}{4}$	$21\frac{7}{8}$	$-\frac{1}{4}$
24	$13\frac{1}{2}$	Conrac	.40	2.7	14	86	15	$24\frac{1}{2}$	15	....
$25\frac{7}{8}$	$20\frac{7}{8}$	ConsEd	2.12	8.6	6	1607	$24\frac{3}{4}$	$24\frac{1}{2}$	$24\frac{3}{4}$	$+\frac{1}{4}$
$44\frac{3}{4}$	37	ConE	pf 5	13.	..	13	$40\frac{1}{8}$	40	40	$+\frac{3}{8}$
$29\frac{5}{8}$	20	ConFd	sk30	4.6	9	503	$28\frac{3}{4}$	$28\frac{1}{4}$	$28\frac{1}{4}$	$-\frac{1}{2}$
$61\frac{1}{4}$	$43\frac{3}{4}$	CnsFrt	2	4.2	10	786	$47\frac{3}{4}$	$47\frac{3}{4}$	$47\frac{3}{4}$	....
$37\frac{7}{8}$	$26\frac{1}{4}$	CnsNG	2.16	6.8	8	239	36	$35\frac{1}{2}$	$35\frac{3}{4}$	....
$21\frac{1}{8}$	$5\frac{7}{8}$	ConsPw	1.40	17.	2	985	$8\frac{1}{4}$	8	$8\frac{1}{8}$	....
$36\frac{1}{2}$	$19\frac{1}{2}$	CnPw	pf4.50	20.	..	z200	23	23	23	$+1\frac{3}{4}$
$54\frac{1}{2}$	$32\frac{1}{2}$	CnPw	pf4.52	14.	..	z30	32	d32	32	$-\frac{2}{4}$
$62\frac{1}{2}$	$29\frac{1}{4}$	CnPw	pf7.45	20.	..	z960	38	37	38	$+\frac{1}{2}$
$64\frac{3}{8}$	29	CnPw	pf7.72	21.	..	z1040	$37\frac{5}{8}$	$36\frac{1}{2}$	37	$+\frac{1}{2}$

The price of each ConsEd share went up $\frac{1}{4}$ point, or 25 cents, from the price it commanded at the close of business the day before.

At the close of the trading day ConsEd shares sold for $24\frac{3}{4}$, or \$24.75 each.

High price for 52 weeks was \$25.87½.

Low price for 52 weeks was \$20.87½.

ConsEd paid 2.12, or \$2.12 per share in dividends.

The percentage yield shows the dividend as a percentage of the share price – in this case 8.6 per cent.

Number of shares (in hundreds) traded in one day. 160,700 shares of ConsEd were traded on this particular day.[1]

[1]The volume of trading may give you a clue to developing trends. For example, if the stock market is down on heavy volume, it may mean that investors are selling before prices fall even further – a strong 'bearish' sign.

[2]Stocks in the same industry tend to have p/e ratios that are roughly the same. A high p/e ratio is not necessarily good or bad, it is only significant in relation to other companies' p/e ratios. If the p/e ratio is significantly below the industry norm, it could either mean that the company is having problems or that it is an undiscovered gem.

4 Compare the performance of your companies with others in the industry. Compare also with an appropriate index (Dow Jones, FT, S and P 500, etc)

5 Present your findings to the class in a short talk (maximum five minutes) and conclude by making investment recommendations.

Section 2

The securities market place

The Commodities Exchange Center, New York

1 Listen to the tape recording of a guide talking to a group of Korean business people at the Commodities Exchange Center (CEC) in downtown Manhattan. Answer the following questions.

1   List the four independent exchanges that trade at the CEC.
2   Where does the trading actually take place at the CEC?
3   One of the CEC's major functions is to fix prices. What is the other?
4   Who are the hedgers?
5   Does a speculator need a large amount of capital in order to invest in futures contracts?
6   Does the speculator generally want to take possession of commodities?
7   How is the price of each contract determined?
8   Which financial futures are mentioned?
9   What is meant by options trading?
10 How do the brokers communicate with each other on the trading floor?
11 How is the latest price information communicated?

2 Fill in the grid below to show the various steps in a commodity transaction.

Person	Action
Customer	
	Transmits the order to the trading floor
	Writes the order on an order ticket
Runner	
	Notes the details of the trade
Runner	Returns order ticket to phone clerk
Phone clerk	
Phone clerk	Reports execution of trade back to broker

8.2.B
Functions

Explaining and giving instructions

Explain one of the following activities to your partner.

- how to buy stocks
- how to withdraw cash from an electronic cash point
- how to programme a VCR
- how to copy information from one computer disk to another
- how to make an international call from a public phone
- how to enrol at a university
- how to prepare for an overseas assignment.

You may find the following expressions useful:

- First of all ...
- Be careful not to ...
- Don't forget to ...
- Make sure you ...
- The _____ works as follows ...
- If you don't _____ you'll ...

- You('ll) have to ...
- You ought to ...
- You should ...
- You must ...

8.2.C
Reading

The London Stock Exchange

I Read the following text about the London Stock Exchange and take notes on the following points:

- its origins
- its functions
- the Big Bang.

The London Stock Exchange is a marketplace – indeed, it is one of the most important markets for stocks and bonds in the world. Like many other famous British institutions, the Stock Exchange was not created overnight; no edict or constitution brought it into being. It developed stage by stage, adapting as it did so to changing economic conditions and needs.

In the seventeenth century, trading firms and governments needed to raise money for their expanding activities – more money than they could obtain from their usual sources. They did this by issuing stocks and shares and inviting the public to buy them. This provided the necessary capital. If the company made a profit, the shareholders received a share of it. If the shareholders wanted to get back the money they had invested, it was not possible to go to the company and ask for it. Instead they had to find somebody interested in buying the shares from them.

A regular market therefore began to form. At first, the brokers used to meet at the Royal Exchange. Then, in the eighteenth century they began to meet in London coffee houses where business was carried out over a cup of coffee or a glass of madeira wine.

In 1773, the market moved to a building of its own and the volume of trade increased steadily so that the London Stock Exchange became the largest in the world and remained so until the First World War.

During the Industrial Revolution, other share markets had developed in other parts of the country, but by 1973 they had amalgamated to form the Stock Exchange of Great Britain and Ireland, and celebrated the event by moving into a brand new tower block in the heart of the City of London.

The next milestone in the history of the Exchange was on 27 October 1986 in an event which came to be known as the Big Bang. Basically, the Big Bang was a deregulation of the Stock Exchange. Until then, the Stock Exchange had been operating a system of restrictive practices under which, for example, it was virtually impossible for foreigners to become members of the Stock Exchange. It was a little like a very exclusive club whereby members could choose who would and who wouldn't be allowed membership rights. Obviously this absence of real competition led, amongst other things, to the members charging their customers higher commissions than would otherwise have been the case.

So, the first major change which the Big Bang brought about was the opening up of the Stock Exchange to outsiders. This was done by ending the distinction between brokers (who execute transactions on behalf of their customers) and jobbers (who buy and sell on their own account to make a market in one or more stocks). Secondly, the Stock Exchange ended the practice of fixed minimum commissions on transactions. This means that investors are now free to negotiate commissions with traders.

The consequences of these changes are far-reaching. Firstly, the difference between trading on the floor and off the floor has been eliminated. In fact much of the trading has now been moved off the trading floor. This has been helped, of course, by the greatly increased use of electronic trading. In the long-term this trend may lead to the London Stock Exchange becoming less important as investors will be able to make their own markets by dealing with each other directly either by phone or by computer.

Secondly, the admission of outsiders has led to a flood of foreign institutions moving into the City. Japanese and American banks, in particular, have been attracted because in both the US and Japan there are laws which ban commercial banks from dealing in stocks. Faced with overwhelming competition from such institutional investment giants as America's Salomon or Japan's Nomura, some much smaller British firms are in danger of being crushed on their own territory. Others are managing to survive by concentrating their resources on the specialities they can excel in.

In spite of these changes, the City has benefited and will continue to benefit from the Big Bang. The high concentration of foreign institutions could transform the City into the hub of a new worldwide computer-linked network of dealers trading US, Western European and Japanese and American stocks independently of any exchange floor. London is, of course, the natural centre for such a network because of its geographical location within a time zone that suits both Japanese and American traders. Also, British tax officers are not too curious about foreigners' financial affairs. There is also a tremendous pool of talent in London, with a lot of people who know how to trade in world markets. And, last but not least, London is the natural choice because of the fact that English is commonly used throughout the world.

2 Design a one-page overhead transparency which could be used to accompany an oral presentation of this information.

<table>
<tr><td>8.2.D
Presenting</td><td>

Presenting an organisation

In small groups, prepare and present a short talk (five minutes maximum) on an organisation of your choice (a company, school, university, trade union, etc). In the very limited time you have available, try and cover the following points:

- its origins
- its activities
- a recent important event.

</td></tr>
</table>

8.2.E

Listening

Yesterday's trading at the London Stock Exchange

Listen to the account of yesterday's trading and say what happened or is happening to the following:

- Wall Street
- US employment data
- UK equities yesterday
- UK equities in the short-term
- fund managers
- sterling
- UK base rates
- Footsie
- yesterday's trading.

8.2.F

Grammar

Linking sentences

Fill in each of the gaps below by using one of the following conjunctions:

nevertheless	so as	which	so
as soon as	by the time	prior to	during
but	subsequently	because	as
although	before	despite	in addition

1 We put our money in property, _____ the property market crashed _____ we lost practically everything.

2 _____ we came into an inheritance, we decided to buy some shares _____ to have a nest egg for our old age.

3 _____ our house was paid for I wanted to speculate _____ my husband had warned me against it.

4 _____ going bankrupt three times, she started up a new company _____ is doing extremely well.

5 She got her MBA and _____ got herself a job on Wall Street _____ meeting her husband.

6 _____ your stay in London, I'd like you to get in touch with Sir Richard Grant in Kensington _____ he could prove to be a useful contact.

7 _____ the Stock Market had begun trading, it was almost too late. _____ , we did manage to sell at a fairly reasonable price.

8 _____ his departure, he left this note for you. _____ , he asked me to thank you.

Accounting

Terms and concepts

9.1.A

Reading

The main concepts and documents

Read the following passage and answer the questions which follow it.

Businesses measure their financial performance by recording and classifying sales, purchases and other transactions, They then present this information in a way which makes it possible to evaluate their past, present and future performance. The various accounting activities are usually divided into two distinct parts: financial accounting and management accounting.

Financial accounting is concerned with preparing information for users outside the organisation. For example, suppliers, banks and other lenders may want to know about the company's profit potential; government agencies are concerned with regulating the business and collecting taxes.

Management accounting, on the other hand, is designed to meet the needs of a particular company. These range from analysing costs – so that management knows exactly how much it costs to produce a given product and how well the business is performing – to financial planning, which involves forecasting sales, costs, expenses and profits and which enables management to spot problems and opportunities, and allocate resources rationally by developing a budget.

Financial accounting is carried out by public accountants who are responsible for auditing the company's financial statements. These are called chartered accountants in the UK. They are independent of the business and provide an objective analysis of the statements before reporting them to shareholders, investors or tax officials. They also provide other financial services including management consulting and tax accounting.

Management accounting is carried out by private accountants who are usually either employed or hired by the business itself or in certain cases by a government agency to supervise the company's accounting system and book-keeping staff and to generate and interpret financial reports.

Book-keepers represent the most routine accounting function of recording all transactions (sales, purchases, loans, wage payments, etc). The highest-ranking financial accountants typically have the title of Controller or Financial Vice-President, and spend their time monitoring and cross-checking all financial data so that top management can be certain that the company is using assets to best advantage.

All companies use an accounting system that records every transaction affecting assets (things which the company owns) and liabilities (things which the company owes). However, within a short period of time the numerous transactions recorded by a book-keeper are likely to mount up. In order to simplify the situation, accountants summarise the transactions by preparing a number of financial statements, the three most important of which are:

- the balance sheet
- the income statement (profit and loss account)
- the statement of changes in financial position (cash flow forecast).

Accountants in the UK have to prepare a further document called the Statement of Source and Application of Funds.

The balance sheet

The balance sheet is prepared at least once a year, at the end of either the calendar year or the fiscal year. It is often referred to as a picture of a company's financial position frozen at a given moment in time, and shows where the company's money came from (liabilities and owners' equity) and where it went to (assets). Figure 20 shows a simplified balance sheet in both American and British layouts. A glossary of terms appears on the next page.

Figure 20:
Balance sheet for Sunshine Wholefoods 31 December 1992

American layout

ASSETS			
Current Assets			
Cash		$22,790	
Marketable securities		4,200	
Accounts receivable	$19,780		
Less: Allowance for doubtful accounts	430	19,350	
Notes receivable		21,500	
Merchandise inventory		12,685	
Prepaid expenses		4,400	
TOTAL CURRENT ASSETS			$84,925
Fixed Assets			
Factory equipment	$64,919		
Less: Accumulated depreciation	11,706	$53,213	
Leasehold improvements	79,345		
Less: Accumulated amortization	14,308	65,037	
TOTAL FIXED ASSETS			£118,250
Intangible Assets			
Organization costs		420	
Trademark		6,405	
Goodwilll		5,000	
TOTAL INTANGIBLE ASSETS			11,825
TOTAL ASSETS			$215,000
LIABILITIES AND SHAREHOLDERS' EQUITY			
Current Liabilities			
Accounts payable	$23,790		
Note payable (short term)	15,115		
Salaries payable	7,452		
Taxes payable	6,318		
TOTAL CURRENT LIABILITIES		$52,675	
Long-term Liabilities			
Long-term note payable @ 12%		$53,750	
TOTAL LIABILITIES			$106,425
Shareholders' Equity			
Common stock, 10,000 shares		$43,000	
Retained earnings			
Beginning of the year	26,460		
Current year	39,115	65,575	
TOTAL SHAREHOLDERS' EQUITY			$108,575
TOTAL LIABILITY AND SHAREHOLDERS' EQUITY		$215,000	

	£	£	£
FIXED ASSETS	Cost	Depn	
Tangible Assets			
Leasehold Improvements	79,345	14,308	65,037
Factory Equipment	64,919	11,706	53,213
	144,264	26,014	118,250
Intangible Assets			
Organisation Costs		420	
Trademark		6,405	
Goodwill		5,000	
			11,825
			130,075
CURRENT ASSETS			
Trade Investments		4,200	
Stock		12,685	
Bills Receivable		21,500	
Trade debtors		19,350	
Prepaid Expenses		4,400	
Bank Balances		22,790	
		84,925	
CREDITORS: AMOUNTS PAYABLE WITHIN ONE YEAR			
Trade Creditors		23,790	
Bills Payable		15,115	
Corporation Tax		6,318	
Other Creditors		7,452	
		52,675	
NET CURRENT ASSETS			32,250
			162,325
CREDITORS: AMOUNTS PAYABLE IN MORE THAN ONE YEAR			
Long Term Loan			53,750
			£108,573
SHARE CAPITAL AND RESERVES			
Issued Share Capital			
43,000 ordinary shares of £1 each			43,000
Profit and Loss Account			65,575
			£108,575

British layout

Glossary

current assets	:	Resources that can be converted into cash within one year
cash	:	Funds on hand or in bank accounts or savings accounts, and which can be withdrawn at short notice.
marketable securities	:	Any investment readily convertible into cash.
accounts receivable	:	Amounts owed by customers.
allowance for doubtful accounts	:	Some accounts receivable are unlikely to be paid and are therefore deducted.
notes receivable	:	Written and signed promises by customers to pay a stated sum on a certain date. The customer's bank is usually responsible for collection.
inventory	:	Assets tied up in things to be eventually sold – raw materials, goods in process (work in progress) and finished goods.
prepaid expenses	:	Services paid for but not yet used and which can be cancelled and turned into cash.
fixed assets	:	Resources you intend to keep, such as buildings, and which you need to run your business.
depreciation	:	The spreading out of the cost of a tangible asset over its useful life. For intangible assets the equivalent accounting procedure is called amortisation. Land is the only fixed asset which does not depreciate.
intangible assets	:	Assets having no physical existence but which can be licensed or sold to others.
goodwill	:	An intangible asset which corresponds to a company's reputation. When a business is purchased, goodwill represents the difference between the company's face value and the price that the purchaser is willing to pay.
current liabilities	:	Debts that the company will have to pay within one year.
accounts payable	:	Accounts that have to be paid within 30 days, usually to suppliers who have offered 30 days credit.
notes payable	:	Written and signed promises to pay a creditor a stated sum on a certain date.
accrued expenses	:	Expenses incurred but for which bills have not yet been received or recorded. Wages and salaries are examples of accrued expenses.
long-term liabilities	:	Debts that fall due more than a year after the balance sheet has been drawn up.
owner's equity	:	The figure which appears on the balance sheet represents the amount raised by the shareholders when the stock was issued.
retained earnings	:	All previous earnings minus the amount distributed as dividends.

The income statement (profit and loss account)

The income statement (US) or profit and loss (P & L) account (UK) is a kind of financial history book which summarises the company's financial operations over a period of time, usually one year. By subtracting all expenses from all revenues the income statement shows the company's net income at the end of the period. This net income is the company's profit and loss. By comparing net income for one year with net income for previous years, owners, creditors and investors can form judgements about the firm's past performance and future prospects. A simplified income statement in both British and American layouts is shown in Figure 21.

Figure 21:
Income statement (profit and loss account) for Sunshine Wholefoods 31 December 1992

American layout

Revenues		
Gross sales		$478,293
Less: Returns and allowances		3,079
Less: Discounts		1,200
NET SALES		$474,014
COST OF GOODS SOLD		
Beginning inventory		£10,473
Purchases for the year	$198,267	
Less: Purchase discounts	5,300	
Net purchases		192,967
Cost of goods available for sale		£203,440
Less: Ending inventory		12,685
COST OF GOODS SOLD		190,755
Gross Profit		$283,259
Operating Expenses		
Selling expenses		
Wages	$101,700	
Advertising	18,075	
Store supplies	24,016	
Payroll taxes	10,170	
Rent	31,142	
Repairs and maintenance	7,418	
Auto and truck	11,697	
Insurance	4,068	
Utilities	8,700	
Depreciation and amortization	13,245	
Miscellaneous	400	
TOTAL SELLING EXPENSES		$230,631
General expenses		
Professional services	$3,916	
Office supplies	1,354	
Miscellaneous	300	
TOTAL GENERAL EXPENSES		$5,570
TOTAL OPERATING EXPENSES		$236,201
		£47,058
Other Income and Expenses		
Interest expense	$4,750	
Interest income	(986)	
TOTAL OTHER INCOME AND EXPENSES		3,764
PRE-TAX PROFIT		$43,294
INCOME TAXES		4,179
		$39,115

British layout

	£	£	£
Turnover (net of Returns)			475,214
Less: Cost of Sales			
Opening Stock		10,473	
Purchases		198,267	
		208,740	
Closing Stock		12,685	
			196,055
GROSS PROFIT			297,159
Selling and Distribution Expenses			
Wages	111,870		
Advertising	18,075		
Packing Materials	24,016		
Motor Expenses	11,697		
Miscellaneous	400		
		166,058	
Overhead Expenses			
Rent and Rates	31,142		
Repairs and Maintenance	7,418		
Insurances	4,068		
Light and Heat	8,700		
Professional fees	3,916		
Office Supplies	1,354		
Miscellaneous	300		
Depreciation	13,245		
Discounts Allowed	1,200		
Discounts Received	(5,300)		
Bank Interest Paid	4,750		
		70,793	
			236,851
NET OPERATING PROFIT			42,308
Bank Deposit Interest Received			986
NET PROFIT before Tax			43,294
Corporation Tax			4,179
NET PROFIT after Tax			39,115
RETAINED EARNINGS brought forward			26,460
RETAINED EARNINGS carried forward			£65,575

The statement of changes in financial position (cash flow forecast)

The statement of changes in financial position (US) or cash flow forecast (UK) shows the sources and uses of an organisation's cash during an accounting period. If the balance sheet is a picture of the company's present situation, and the P & L account its history book, then the cash flow forecast can be described as the company's crystal ball offering projection of the company's future activities. It is extremely useful for analysing whether future operations will provide enough cash to cover expenses or whether the company will need to turn to other sources of financing.

1 What is the difference between:

- financial accounting and management accounting?
- public accountants and private accountants?
- a controller and a book-keeper?
- assets and liabilities?
- the P & L account and the cash flow forecast?

2 Match the following US and UK terms.

US	UK
1 Statement of changes in financial position	**a** Finance Director
2 Income statement	**b** Fixed asset investments
3 Financial Vice-President	**c** Cash flow forecast
4 Public accountants	**d** Bills of exchange payable
5 Marketable securities	**e** Trade creditors
6 Accounts receivable	**f** Chartered accountants
7 Accounts payable	**g** Inventory stock
8 Notes payable	**h** P & L account
9 Merchandise inventory	**i** Trade debtors
10 CEO	**j** Managing Director

3 By referring to the documents presented on pages 110 and 112, explain how the following amounts are arrived at. The first one has been done for you.

  a Gross profit: *net sales minus cost of goods sold*
  b Net income:
  c Pre-tax profit:
  d Net profit:
  e Total assets:
  f Total shareholders' equity:

Defining key terms

1 Match the following terms with their definitions:

Terms

1 financial accounting
2 management accounting
3 budget
4 public accountants
5 private accountants
6 audit
7 assets
8 liabilities
9 balance sheet
10 goodwill
11 income statement
12 book-keepers
13 controllers
14 accounts receivable
15 depreciation
16 cash flow forecast

Definitions

a concerned with preparing information for internal use
b a financial blueprint of estimated revenues and expenses for a given period of time
c people involved in record-keeping and other clerical jobs in accounting
d a financial statement showing the sources and uses of an organisation's cash during an accounting period
e concerned with preparing information for outside users
f evaluation of the accuracy and reliability of a company's financial statements
g statement of a firm's assets, liabilities and owners' equity at a specific moment in time
h the highest-ranking accountant in a firm
i the spreading out of a tangible asset's cost over its estimated useful life
j accountants who are independent of the organisations they serve
k the value of a business's reputation
l valuable things owned by a company
m debts or obligations the company owes
n accountants employed by a business to supervise the accounting system
o amounts due from customers
p statement showing the firm's overall profitability

2 Divide into two teams. Each member of each team reads aloud a definition and asks one member of the opposing team to give the corresponding term. The person answering must not consult his or her notes and has five seconds to answer in order to earn a point.

Vocabulary

Classifying

Make a copy of the grid below and place the following items in it.

1 three trucks
2 a patent on a new process devised by Calypso Potteries plc
3 12 tons of clay
4 interest due on a bank loan
5 mortgage
6 10,000 shares in the company
7 a lap-top computer for the CEO
8 taxes
9 a 'Calypso' trademark
10 three industrial kilns
11 an unpaid invoice for 600 dishes purchased last month by a Swedish department store
12 the lease on a warehouse
13 money in the company safe for day-to-day expenses
14 the copyright for the series of Calypso publications *Pottery through the ages*
15 unpaid invoice for last week's clay delivery
16 the unexpired portion of an insurance policy

Calypso Potteries plc	
Current assets	Current liabilities
Fixed assets	Long-term liabilities
Intangible assets	Shareholders' equity

Project

Drawing up a balance sheet and income statement

From the following information prepare a balance sheet and an income statement (US layout).

	$
Gross sales	2,000,000
Returns and discounts on sales	50,000
Cash	100,000
Purchases	1,400,000
Purchase returns and discounts	200,000
Equipment	1,000,000
Building and land	2,000,000
Mortgage on building and land	1,500,000
Beginning merchandise inventory	200,000
Ending merchandise inventory	300,000
Accounts receivable	250,000
Accounts payable	200,000
Office supplies	25,000
Selling expenses	200,000
Advertising expenses	400,000
General administration expenses	200,000
Retained earnings	1,475,000
Owner's equity	375,000
Accrued wages payable	100,000

Section 2

Creative accounting

Summarising 1

Avoiding plagiarism

Plagiarism is presenting another person's words or ideas as if they were your own. Although occasionally intentional, it is more often due to the writer being unaware of what constitutes plagiarism. However, whether deliberate or accidental, plagiarism is seriously frowned upon in business, education, research, and in general.

It is therefore essential to document the following:

- direct quotations
- opinions and judgements of the original author
- facts that are not widely known, or universally accepted
- statistical data.

The following passage is an extract from an article which appeared in *The Economist*. Following the passage are five summaries, four of which are guilty of plagiarism. In each of these cases identify the specific violations of the plagiarism guidelines above.

Discounting for creativity

Pensions-contribution holidays, use and abuse of provisions, capitalisation of costs, changes of depreciation policy, "extraordinary" losses taken below the line but profits deemed merely "exceptional" and therefore above it; these are just some of the (quite lawful) accounting mechanisms that can make earnings and their quality a matter of judgement rather than fact. The London office of UBS Phillips & Drew deserves investors' thanks, but will not earn much love from the nearly 200 big British companies whose accounts it studied, for drawing pointed attention to them.

In a pamphlet, "Accounting for Growth", the researchers list, for instance, 20 companies that have convertible bonds with put options, This was a wondrous mid 1980s mechanism for raising supercheap money. But if the firm's share price collapses, it can – ask Saatchi & Saatchi – become a horrendous liability. Generally, this should be provided against – which, of course, cuts reported profits. Not all the 20 do provide; some with good reason, some less so. One group, LIG, has just bitten the bullet and launched a £62m ($118m) rights issue to ensure it has the money when it is needed. At least two other names on the list could one day be reaching for their pockets–or those of their shareholders.

The Economist, 19 January 1991

Summary 1

There are many accounting mechanisms which accountants can use, quite legally, in order to make the company's position look healthier. Using different methods of calculating depreciation, for example, or capitalisation of costs are commonly used ploys.

Many big British companies have convertible bonds with put options which could prove costly if share prices fall. Accountants' failure to provide against this possibility could mean that shareholders will one day have a nasty shock.

Summary 2

There are many accounting mechanisms which accountants can use, quite legally, in order to make the company's position look healthier. Using different methods of calculating depreciation, for example, or capitalisation of costs are commonly used ploys.

Many big British companies have convertible bonds with put options which could prove costly if share prices fall. Accountants' failure to provide against this possibility means that some companies could one day be reaching for their pockets – or those of their shareholders.

Discounting for creativity – The Economist (19/01/91)

Summary 3

There are many accounting mechanisms which accountants can use, quite legally, in order to make the company's position look healthier. Using different methods of calculating depreciation, for example, or capitalisation of costs are commonly used ploys.

Many big British companies have convertible bonds with put options which could prove costly if share prices fall. Accountants' failure to provide against this possibility could mean that shareholders will one day have a nasty shock.

Discounting for creativity – The Economist (19/01/91)

Summary 4

There are many accounting mechanisms which accountants can use, quite legally, in order to make the company's position look healthier. Using different methods of calculating depreciation, for example, or capitalisation of costs are commonly used ploys.

Many big British companies have 'convertible bonds with put options'[1] which could prove costly if share prices fall. Accountants' failure to provide against this possibility could mean that shareholders will one day have a nasty shock.

[1]*Discounting for creativity – The Economist* (19/01/91)

Summary 5

There are many accounting mechanisms which unscrupulous accountants can use in order to make the company's position look healthier. Using different methods of calculating depreciation, for example, or capitalisation of costs are commonly used ploys.

Many big British companies have convertible bonds with put options which could prove costly if share price fall. Accountants' failure to provide against this possibility could mean that shareholders will one day have a nasty stock.

Discounting for creativity – The Economist (19/01/91)

9.2.B
Summarising 2

Being brief and to the point

Read the following passage and then write a summary of it in no more than 70 words.

MEASUREMENT OF PROFITABILITY

It has been argued that profitability is the primary aim and the best measure of efficiency in competitive business. However, profits as such are meaningless unless related to the equity (ordinary) shareholders' investment in the business. The relationship between the capital invested in a business and the profits earned is the rate of return on capital employed. The ability to earn a satisfactory rate of return on equity shareholders' investment is the most important characteristic of the successful business. Increased sales volume is at best a short-term indication of successful growth, and, without additional information, must be viewed as such.

In the long run, increased sales volume may prove a deceptive guidepost if there is not a proper return on the capital necessary to support these sales. Real growth comes from the ability of management to employ successfully additional capital at a satisfactory rate of return. This is the final criterion of the soundness and strength of a company's growth, for in a competitive economy capital gravitates towards the more profitable enterprises. The company that is merely expanding sales at a declining rate of return on capital employed will eventually be unable to attract expansion capital. Thus any measurement of a company's effectiveness must be based on the successful employment of capital.

J Sizer, *An Insight into Management Accounting*, Pelican (1975)

9.2.C
Vocabulary

Verbs and nouns in context

I All of the following verbs appear in this unit. Insert them in the gaps in the sentences below, conjugating them wherever necessary.

to record	to allocate	to owe
to tie up	to incur	to classify
to design	to provide	to mount up
to withdraw	to forecast	to spot
to carry out	to affect	to depreciate

1 It was lucky she _____ the mistake before the documents went up to the controller's office.

2 We've run out of cash. Could you go the bank and _____ $150?

3 The management has just decided _____
more resources to the R&D department.

4 We shouldn't _____ too much of our capital
in inventory.

5 He was concerned about how the new law _____
our accounting procedures.

6 We've _____ heavy losses but the prospects
for next year are much better.

7 Our accounting system is _____ to tightly
control costs.

8 Unpaid bills have _____ on his desk since he
went on sick leave.

9 They're slow payers; they still _____ us over
$100 from the January order.

10 It's going to be tricky _____ expenses when
we're not even sure about next quarter's sales.

11 I would like you _____ an objective analysis of
the situation.

12 Property around here will never _____ . It will
probably double in value over the next five years.

13 Last year she _____ a three-month accounting
traineeship with Maple Leaf Enterprises.

14 It is essential for the company's book-keepers _____
and _____ every transaction made.

2 Find the nouns which correspond to the following verbs.

Example

> to install → an installation

1 to record	9 to generate	17 to appear
2 to classify	10 to interpret	18 to summarise
3 to present	11 to simplify	19 to subtract
4 to evaluate	12 to convert	20 to project
5 to perform	13 to withdraw	21 to state
6 to lend	14 to pay	22 to involve
7 to regulate	15 to deduct	23 to calculate
8 to allocate	16 to depreciate	24 to capitalise

3 Fill in the blanks in the following paragraph, using nouns from the previous
exercise.

Here is a _____1_____ of the Chairman's
_____2_____ regarding the company's
_____3_____ for the second quarter. In spite of new government _____4_____ , sales increased by 8%, leading to
the _____5_____ of higher profits. Although the
_____6_____ of sterling has led us to revise our
_____7_____ for the coming year, the
_____8_____ of an extra half a million dollars to the
advertising budget and the _____9_____ of our production process mean that next year we'll beat every _____10_____ .

Compound words

Vocabulary

1 Match each of the words in the first column with words in the second column to make compound nouns.

1	cross	**a**	sheet
2	finished	**b**	expenses
3	accrued	**c**	receivable
4	cash	**d**	statement
5	crystal	**e**	costs
6	accounts	**f**	earnings
7	current	**g**	ball
8	notes	**h**	capital
9	rights	**i**	goods
10	balance	**j**	taxes
11	income	**k**	check
12	income	**l**	flow
13	working	**m**	issue
14	production	**n**	payable
15	retained	**o**	assets
16	fiscal	**p**	year

2 Write a concise definition for three of the above terms *without using a dictionary* and without using the term itself. In small groups, read your definitions to each other. The other members of your group have to decide which term you are defining.

Section 3

Controlling the cash flow

Complaints, apologies and excuses

Listening

1 Listen to the tape recording of five conversations. Make a copy of the grid on the next page and fill it in as you listen.

	Complaint	Excuse given	Resolution of problem
Conversation 1			
Conversation 2			
Conversation 3			
Conversation 4			
Conversation 5			

2 Reply to each of the following complaints by *apologising* and giving an appropriate *excuse*.

Example

> **Complaint:** We ordered 40 cases of felt-tips and you've only sent us 14.
> **Excuse:** I'm sorry about that, but there must have been a misunderstanding.
> *or* Please accept our apologies. The problem may have been due to keyboard error.

Complaints

1 We ordered the goods 17 days ago and we've still not received them.
2 We've just received the consignment and part of it is missing.
3 You sent the order to 171 Broad Street. Our address is 71 Broad Street.
4 Mr Smith did tell me he'd phone early in the week but I've still not heard from him.
5 Listen, you've kept me holding on for over five minutes.
6 I've been trying to get through to your accounts department all day but the line's always busy.

3 Look at the previous exercise again. This time, after you have given your excuse, try to resolve the problem. The following expressions may be helpful.

- I'll get him to deal with it.
- I'll get our transport department to deliver it straightaway.
- I'll look into it immediately.
- I'll ask one of our representatives to call in this week.
- I'll deal with it myself.
- Could you leave this with me and I'll call you back this afternoon?

Case study

Controlling cash flow

Read the following case study and then answer the questions which follow it.

Regal Leather is a small up-and-coming company producing top-quality leather bags and briefcases. The company has 10 workers, one Sales Manager and a Managing Director, Vincent Jones, whose responsibilities include looking after the company's accounts. Turnover for last year reached £1,800,000, which represented a 10% increase over the previous year and confirmed Regal Leather's growing importance in the industry. Production capacity for the plant is currently 500 units per week over 48 weeks, plus 10% if overtime is introduced. The plant closes in September for four weeks.

Mr Jones had just finished his morning coffee and was beginning to study the architects' plans for the new production wing when his Sales Manager, John Howard, walked into the office with a letter in his hand. 'Hi, Vincent', he said, 'Here, take a look at this', and he thrust the letter into Mr Jones's outstretched hand. Mr Jones read the letter carefully.

Figure 22:
Letter to Regal Leather

WESTERN EMPORIUM PLC ■ **37 EUSTON SQUARE** ■ **LONDON** ■ **NW1 3D5**
Tel: 071 441 3829 ■ *Fax: 071 442 3773* ■ *Telex: 77470*

20 May 1993

Mr John Howard
Sales Manager
Regal Leather
Aston Triangle
Birmingham B4 832

Dear Mr HOWARD

When I visited your stand at the International Trade Fair in Kensington last month, I was most impressed by the quality of your products and the competitiveness of your prices. We have a number of clients in the Middle East and South East Asia who have expressed a strong interest in this type of quality good.

I would very much like to get together with you within the next few days in order to negotiate terms for the following order:

Quantity	Model	Code	Catalogue price(£)	Total(£)
3,000	Executive briefcase	EB 130	75	225.00
3.600	Travel case	TC 260	75	270.00
				495.00

We would require that the goods be delivered in 3 consignments as follows:
 - the first consignement (2,200 units) no later than 30 June 1993
 - the second consignment (2,200 units) no later than 31 July 1993
 - the third consignment (2.200 units) no later than 31 August 1993.

For an order of this size, we hope that you would be willing to extend your normal 30-day payment period and accept payment on 1st November 1993.

We look forward to hearing from you.

Yours sincerely

James Williamson

James WILLIAMSON
Purchasing Manager

When Mr Jones had finished reading the letter, he put it down, looked up and asked his Sales Manager what he thought of it. 'Great, looks like we've hit a gold-mine', exclaimed Howard. 'Maybe', replied Jones, 'but we might just as easily hit a landmine which blows us into bankruptcy'.

Work in pairs and answer the following questions.

1 Find three reasons to explain Mr Jones's apparent lack of enthusiasm.

2 The cost of meeting Western Emporium's order would be as follows (in pounds sterling):

raw materials	70,000 per month x 3 months	= 210,000
wages and salaries	22,000 per month x 3 months	= 66,000
overtime	2,000 per month x 3 months	= 6,000
overheads	41,000 per month x 3 months	= 123,000
Total	135,000 per month x 3 months	= 405,000

Complete the cash flow forecast below. Receipts of £155,000 and £40,000 in June and July refer to payments for orders delivered in April and May.

Regal Leather: Cash flow forecast						
	June	July	August	Sept	Oct	Nov
Receipts	155,000	40,000				505,000
Payments				63,000	123,000	123,000
Receipts +/– payments						
Opening balance	45,000					
Closing balance						

3 Analyse your completed cash flow forecast and discuss the problems which it raises. Decide what should be done.

4 Draft a letter to Western Emporium, explaining your position.

5 Hand over your completed letter to another pair who will now play the role of Western Emporium plc. When they have read the letter, try to negotiate a solution which suits both parties.

9.3.C
Writing

Requests and reminders

Read the following information about ACL Holdings and then answer the questions which follow.

ACL Holdings is normally a good customer, placing regular orders and settling the invoice within 30 days. However, your accounts department has not yet received payment for a consignment delivered six weeks ago. Figure 23 is a copy of the invoice which was sent to ACL Holdings with the consignment.

Figure 23:
Invoice sent to ACL Holdings

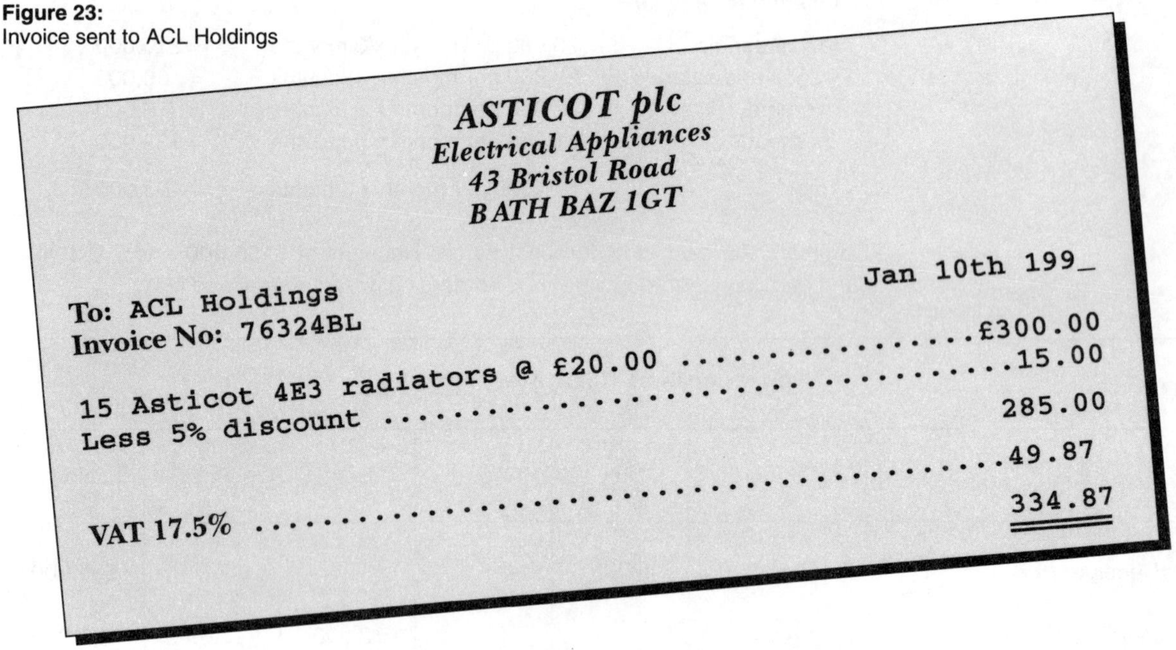

```
                    ASTICOT plc
                  Electrical Appliances
                    43 Bristol Road
                    BATH BAZ 1GT

                                        Jan 10th 199_

To: ACL Holdings
Invoice No: 76324BL                          ..........£300.00

15 Asticot 4E3 radiators @ £20.00 ...............   15.00
Less 5% discount .............................      285.00

                                         ...........  49.87
VAT 17.5% ...............................            334.87
```

1 Write a letter of reminder to ACL Holdings.

2 You work in the accounts department of ACL Holdings. Two of your large customers have just gone into liquidation, leaving their accounts outstanding. This has resulted in a temporary liquidity crisis in your company. Reply to Asticot plc explaining your difficulties and requesting an extension of credit.

COMPANY FOCUS
Financial services at Merrill Lynch

Read the following extracts from the 1991 Annual Report of Merrill Lynch and answer the questions below.

1 Why is the need for individual savings and investments so great? What is Merrill Lynch doing to meet this need?

2 How important are small to mid-sized business and financial institutions to the American economy? List all the services which Merrill Lynch offers these companies.

3 What were the main economic trends of 1991? What services did Merrill Lynch offer its corporate clients?

4 How are sovereign governments reacting to changes in the economic environment?

5 Why is Merrill Lynch important for states and municipalities?

INDIVIDUAL CLIENTS

For more than 50 years, Merrill Lynch has led the way in helping people plan their financial futures and in providing the tools and guidance to build, manage and preserve wealth. Through our Financial Consultants, who we believe are the best trained and most professional in the financial service industry, our company delivers the highest level of advice and counsel – along with superior research, investment products, client service, and the Merrill Lynch 'tradition of trust.'

Our Financial Consultants focus in bringing added value to the investment process and on developing long-term client relationships. As a result, Merrill Lynch is positioned to play an important role in the years ahead, as vast numbers of Americans and others around the world discover a need to save and invest for the future.

In America and elsewhere, people can expect to live longer than ever before. Thus, there has never been more need to save and invest for a comfortable retirement. Nor has it ever been more challenging to finance a child's education, to help with the purchase of a child's first home, or to preserve an estate from one generation to the next.

This is especially critical for the 75 million post-war Baby Boomers now approaching middle age, who do not have the same ingrained habits of saving and investing as their parents.

The Premier Team of Financial Consultants

The key to achieving preeminence in our industry is the Merrill Lynch Financial Consultant. Our FCs, in more than 500 offices in the United States and 28 other countries, are skilled at knowing and anticipating clients' financial needs and at charting the right financial course for each of them.

Our Financial Consultants draw upon the Merrill Lynch specialists in insurance tax and estate planning, trusts and small business. They are supported by Merrill Lynch's highly ranked Global Securities Research Group.

Merrill Lynch clients also benefit from superior products and services. We created such important industry innovations as our pioneering Cash Management Account® (CMA®) and Capital Builder^{SM} Account (CBA®), and we have the leading market share in accounts of these types. Merrill Lynch clients can choose from a wide array of professional money management services, including more than 120 investment portfolios managed by Merrill Lynch Asset Management (MLAM).

Merrill Lynch remains committed to helping educate clients and the public about financial planning and investing. In 1991, over a million people attended seminars conducted by our Financial Consultants, and Merrill Lynch published and distributed extensive educational materials through mailings, seminars, our branch offices and the media.

All of this explains why people put their trust in Merrill Lynch. During 1991, total assets in Merrill Lynch client accounts rose 17% to $435 billion – equivalent to an increase of $242 million per business day. The funds in these accounts represent almost 2.5% of all U.S. household financial assets.

SMALL TO MID-SIZE BUSINESSES AND FINANCIAL INSTITUTIONS

Merrill Lynch understands the challenges of both expanding and mature businesses. And we also are committed to helping their owners and managers on an individual level. Our firm takes special pride in serving the distinctive needs of small to mid-size businesses and financial institutions. They represent the fastest growing sector of the U.S. economy, accounting for more than 90% of all new jobs created during 1991.

Merrill Lynch Business Financial Services is a unique team of professionals dedicated to helping these companies thrive in the years ahead, with innovative financial products and services that give entrepreneurs and managers of smaller companies the same tools available to larger organizations.

Working in concert with Merrill Lynch Financial Consultants, our professionals provide a range of services from cash management, financing and retirement planning to evaluating a mature business and developing a plan for its disposition. At the end of 1991, nearly 400,000 small to mid-size businesses and financial institutions had entrusted Merrill Lynch with more than $77 million in assets, an increase of nearly 20% over 1990.

In addition, through Merrill Lynch International Inc., our firm provides selected companies with equity, mezzanine and senior financing.

Efficient Cash Management and Financing

Efficient management of working capital is critical to every business. To make the most of their valuable capital, increasing numbers of businesses are turning to Merrill Lynch's powerful cash management tool, the Working Capital Management^{SM} account (WCMS®). The number of these accounts increased 12% in 1991 to more than 100,000 while assets in WCMA and other business accounts increased 17% to more than $32 billion.

The WCMA account is superior to other business asset accounts in that it combines all the necessary elements for effective cash management. By combining business checking, borrowing, investing, funds transfer services and charge card processing into a single account, the WCMA frees business owners and managers from many day-to-day cash management chores, giving them more time for hands-on business activities.

Moreover, the WCMA account helps businesses bring more revenue to the bottom line by automatically paying down outstanding loans and sweeping excess cash into a variety of money market funds. In 1991, WCMA account began offering electronic charge card processing to retail merchants, chain stores, medical groups and other professional service providers throughout the U.S.

Merrill Lynch's superior financial strength has enabled us to continue meeting the borrowing needs of small and mid-size businesses at a time when many traditional lenders are reducing their commitments.

LARGE CORPORATIONS AND INSTITUTIONAL CLIENTS

Merrill Lynch's goal is to render the highest level of service to our corporate clients in helping them meet all of their financing and strategic objectives. In 1991, our leadership in virtually all facets of the global capital markets – in origination, trading, research and distribution – enabled us to achieve this goal during one of the greatest market surges in history.

The year began with the onset of the Gulf War in January and saw the Dow Jones Industrial Average rise from 2,633 to 3,168 by year's end. The NASDAQ Composite Index rose by 57%, and short-term interest rates fell to levels unseen since the 1970s. Corporations around the world rushed to refund high coupon debt and raise additional debt and equity. Worldwide debt and equity financing activity exceeded $868 billion, an increase of 65% over 1990.

Merrill Lynch helped its issuing clients achieve their objectives in this favorable environment. Moreover, while the pace of structural change slowed in various world economies – as measured by reduced mergers and acquisition activity – Merrill Lynch continued to be of service in advising clients on acquisitions, divestitures, joint ventures and similar ways of implementing strategic plans.

SOVEREIGN GOVERNMENTS

The capital needs of sovereign governments and supranational organizations worldwide continue to grow, as governments everywhere position their economies to compete in a new environment of liberalized cross-border trade and capital flows. With our strengths in global and domestic capital markets, Merrill Lynch is ideally suited to meet these client needs for financial advisory and underwriting services – to help them in obtaining the lowest-cost capital and in privatizing their state-owned industries.

Privatizations

Heightened global competition continues to accelerate the sweep toward privatization of gov-ernment-owned industries in many parts of the world. Merrill Lynch remains a leader in providing advisory and investment banking services for privatizations worldwide. In fact, we are among the few firms with a leadership position in all the services and market segments needed to evaluate, plan and execute successful privatizations in all regions of the world.

Our broad range of skills includes:
- Financial advisory expertise
- Mergers and acquisitions capability
- Restructing and advisory experience
- Equity and debt training, underwriting, and distribution capability
- Broad and respected global research.

MUNICIPAL FINANCE

As a leader in municipal finance, with an individual and institutional investor base that has a strong need for tax-saving municipal securities, Merrill Lynch is helping states, municipalities and their political subdivisions solve their most challenging funding needs. During the year, Merrill Lynch lead-managed 339 new municipal issues totaling $16.3 billion, for a nearly 10% market share.

To give tax-exempt borrowers greater access to the capital markets at lower cost, Merrill Lynch introduced Floating Auction Tax-Exempts[SM]/ Residual Interest Tax-Exempt[SM] Securities, or FLOAT[SM]/RITES[SM]. These securities, by appealing to both short- and long-term investors, combine to produce an all-in fixed rate of 10 to 30 basis points below traditional long-term fixed-rate alternatives.

Answers, tapescripts and notes for teachers

UNIT 1

1.1.B

1 Posting vacancies on the company noticeboard; employee magazines; referrals from superiors; consulting the company's data base and employee files.
2 To inject new blood from time to time (new ideas, different perspectives); to introduce new skills into the company.
3 Organisations where there is a shortage of trained people (example from student's countries?).

1.1.C

Suggested answers
Posting: displaying – The final grades will be posted/posted up on Friday.
Vacancies: jobs available/jobs vacant – We have three vacancies for experienced sales staff.
Subordinate: somebody who has a less important position in a company – I delegate all the routine work to my subordinates.
Files: a collection of information about a particular person or thing – Get me the IBM file, please.
Data base: a collection of data stored on computer – What kind of information does your company store on its data base?
Fee: money paid for a particular service – The better the university, the higher the tuition fees.
Headhunting: persuading someone to leave their company and work elsewhere – We've become a victim of headhunting; three of our senior executives have just handed in their notice.
Unsolicited applications: spontaneous applications – We don't bother advertising our vacancies as we receive so many unsolicited applications.

1.1.D

Suggested answers
Company magazine: Advantages – can give complete job description; can be read at leisure; encourages employees to read magazine thereby reinforcing corporate identity. Disadvantage – limited readership.
Data base/files: Advantages – enables company to see at a glance who is best suited for a vacancy; motivating for employees to know that their performance is monitored and possibly rewarded. Disadvantage – Big Brother syndrome.
Speciality publications: Advantages – relevant readership very high; quality image. Disadvantages – long preparation time (especially for quarterly or monthly publications); expensive.
National or regional press: Advantages – wide audience; some socio-professional selectivity. Disadvantages – relevant readership relatively small; cluttered pages.
Radio and television: Advantages – very wide audience, but difficult to target. Disadvantages – expensive; short life of message.
Public agencies: Advantages – free of charge. Disadvantages – not very specialised; inferior image.
Private agencies: Advantages – may offer specific services, including search services and consulting; specialised. Disadvantage – expensive.
Unsolicited applications: Advantages – free; applicants ready for work immediately; applicants have initiative, motivation. Disadvantage – must coincide with vacancy.

1.1.E

Suggested answers
1 Company noticeboard used mainly for low-level positions: press used across the board: radio and television hardly ever used; three principal sources of management recruitment (private agencies, press, search firms); two principal sources of sales personnel recruitment (press, private agencies).
2 A personnel manager could use this information to help choose the most appropriate recruitment source for various categories of employee.
   Extension: Would you expect to see similar data for recruitment in your own country?

1.1.F
1 more; than   2 many; as   3 least used   4 slightly; than   5 least
6 mainly/mostly   7 more than; of   8 insignificant/poor/ineffective
9 slightly fewer   10 twice as   11 half as; as   12 times; many.

1.2.A
1 skilled worker   2 book-keeper   3 PA
4 MD/CEO   5 data base administrator   6 fundraiser
7 clerk   8 unskilled worker   9 shorthand typist
10 PR officer   11 foreman   12 systems analyst.

1.3.A
1 management skills   2 communication skills   3 research skills
4 technical skills   5 teaching skills   6 financial skills
7 creative skills   8 helping skills   9 clerical skills.

1.3.B
1 c   2 h   3 g   4 b   5 d   6 i   7 a   8 f   9 e.
2 1 administration   2 analysis   3 assignment   4 attainment
   5 development   6 execution   7 improvement   8 increase
   9 recommendation   10 strength   11 supervision   12 arrangement
   13 draft   14 speech   15 diagnosis   16 evaluation
   17 assembly   18 building   19 solution   20 training
   21 advice   22 encouragement.
3 1 draft   2 strength   3 speech   4 assembly
   5 assignment   6 encouragement/advice   7 solution
   8 training   9 supervision   10 improvement.

1.3.D
2 Job seekers should choose the style and select the resumé categories that best fit their experience and qualifications. The range of categories is vast – here are some examples:

Education   Education and qualifications
Education and specialised training   Experience
Work experience   Professional experience
Professional experience and skills   Experience and achievements
Employment history   Interests
Outside interests   Activities and interests
Other information   Other facts
Other skills   Honours/awards
Personal data

Extension
This section offers many opportunities for students to explore the cultural dimension (the codes that govern behaviour and the institutions which both shape and reflect mentalities) of English-speaking countries, and for teachers to share their knowledge. The teacher may take the opportunity to introduce students to the educational system in one English-speaking country. For example, Britain's schools and universities, the various exams, the curriculum, extra-curricular activities, public schools and the 'old boy' network, the number of graduates and the breakdown according to subject and so on.

UNIT 2

2.1.A
Suggested answers
1 To choose the person best suited to the job; to reject unsuitable applicants; to investigate aspects of applicant's past record, current skills, future motivation and so on, which could not be investigated by other means; to air any uncertainties and allow applicant to reply; to offer applicant the opportunity to find out more about the company, the position, work conditions and so on.
2 Bad recruitment leads to inefficiency, loss of productivity, etc; replacing somebody is disruptive, bad for team morale, time-consuming and expensive; if you reject a good applicant, he or she may end up working for your competitors; the key to successful business is to employ highly competent people.
3 Properly designed tests can measure a number of variables (which?) but cannot fulfil all the functions listed above.

2.1.D
Suggested answers (other answers must be justified)
Job knowledge: 1; 9
Simulation or situational: 4; 5; 10; 15; 16
Work willingness: 7; 11; 13
Open-ended: 3; 8
Stress interviewing: 2; 6; 12; 14

2.1.E
Suggested answers (variations possible according to culture)
Nervous: 1; 4; 8; 9
Confident: 5; 10
Unsure: 3; 6
Overconfident: 2; 7
1 Other behavioural cues: bowing; yawning; stuttering; smiling; perspiring.

2.2.A

1 1	**2** q	**3** j	**4** c	**5** h	**6** o	**7** e	**8** a	**9** p
10 m	**11** k	**12** d	**13** g	**14** n	**15** i	**16** f	**17** b.	

2.3.C

Graphology (tapescript)

Many companies nowadays use graphologists as part of their selection procedure. Sometimes the graphologist is asked to analyse the applicants' cover letters as soon as they are received, and screen the applicants accordingly. In other cases the graphologist waits until after the interview before asking the applicant to provide a sample of his or her handwriting for analysis.

There are a number of characteristics which graphologists look at to build up a picture of the applicant's personality. The first factor graphologists consider is the layout of the page. They divide up the page spacially so that the bottom of the page symbolises the Earth, while the top symbolises the sky; the left-hand side represents the past, and the right-hand side the future.

If, for example, the writing is very close to the left-hand edge of the sheet, it means the writer is conservative and strongly attached to traditional values. A wide left-hand margin, on the other hand, means the individual hasn't yet reconciled himself with his problematic past; he still has a number of hang-ups about his past. Also, the spaces between the letters of a word and between the words themselves is of major importance. A lot of spaces means a desire to communicate, to go towards others, whereas dense, compact handwriting with very few spaces means a desire to occupy all the space, to be overassertive and overbearing and to put up barriers between oneself and others.

Another important factor is the size of the actual letters. The size of the letters corresponds to the image which the individual has of himself. Small letters mean that he underestimates himself, either through lack of maturity or lack of confidence, or through simple modesty. Large letters, on the other hand, show enthusiasm and exuberance, but in extreme cases reveal vanity and arrogance.

The slope of the lines can be very revealing. Lines which rise show optimism and willpower but if the lines rise very sharply this could mean that the individual is an opportunist or that he's excessive. Lines which fall show sickness, tiredness, depression and lack of self confidence.

Next the graphologist considers the pressure of the pen on the paper. A thick line indicates a warm, extrovert individual whereas a thin line means that the person is more analytic and has more depth. A hesitant line, on the other hand, shows apathy and lack of willpower.

The slope of the letters is another important clue. Upright letters indicate self-control, individualism and a free-thinking nature. Letters which slope forward show curiosity and ease of integration. Backward-sloping letters, on the other hand, indicate difficulties in adapting to new situations and may mean the writer has a suspicious temperament. Writing which is very regular may be a sign of excessive conformity and rigidity.

The graphologist also considers the way the letters are joined. Smooth joins indicate a certain intellectual flexibility and logic. Letters that are badly joined mean that the person needs time to think before he acts.

The speed of the handwriting is another important sign. Rapid writing shows intellectual dynamism although if it's too rapid this could indicate a lack of attention for detail. Slow handwriting is more typical of an analytic individual. Very slow handwriting reveals a certain indolence and lack of energy.

Another very revealing clue is the shape of the letters themselves. Highly stylised, calligraphic handwriting means a lack of personality and an unhealthy obedience to conventions. Simple handwriting without unnecessary ornaments shows that the individual is frank and simple, with above-average intelligence. On the other hand, complicated handwriting with lots of frills and flourishes shows a certain vanity and artificiality. Angular writing with sharp, stiff shapes means that the writer is energetic, but also intransigent. Round letters reveal a happy-go-lucky individual. However, if the round letters such as the 'o', the 'b' or the 'd' are not closed, this may indicate laziness.

2.2.C

Handwriting characteristics		Key words regarding writer's personality
Layout	close to the left wide margin many spaces few spaces	conservative; tradition unreconciled; hang-ups communicative; outgoing overassertive; overbearing; barriers
Size of letters	small letters large letters	underestimation; immature; lacks confidence; modesty enthusiasm; exuberance; vanity; arrogance
Slope of lines	upward sloping (slight) upward sloping (extreme) downward sloping	optimism; willpower opportunist; excessive sickness; tiredness; depression; lack of self-confidence
Pressure	heavy pressure light pressure very light pressure	warm, extrovert analytic; deep apathy; lack of willpower
Slope of letters	upright forward sloping backward sloping very regular	self control; individualism; free-thinking curiosity; ease of integration can't adapt; suspicious conformity; rigidity
Joins between letters	smoothly joined badly joined	intellectual flexibility needs time
Speed	rapid very rapid slow very slow	intellectual dynamism no detail analytic indolence; lack of energy
Shape of letters	calligraphic simple complicated angular round open rounds	lacks personality; obeys conventions frank; simple; intelligent vanity; artificiality energetic; intransigent happy-go-lucky laziness

2.2.E

Methods of recruitment and selection (tapescript)

1st recruiter

I'm Chairman of the Management Department at a large State University; we've got about 60,000 students altogether, 4,000 of whom are currently studying at the College of Business. When I need to recruit a professor for my department, I first have to send a report to the Dean justifying the recruitment. If the Dean gives her go-ahead, I get together a search committee which draws up a job profile. We're obliged by law to post the vacancy internally, and I also place adverts in the leading management journals and reviews.

We might get as many as 30 to 40 applicants for a single vacancy so we then have to sort through the applications and weed out all those who don't have the appropriate background. What we usually do then is phone those people up and advise them that they don't have the right fit. Usually they accept this but if they do insist on an interview anyway, we have to respect their wish as the law forbids us to reject people solely on their written application.

We then send teams of interviewers around the country. The interviewers, who are department faculty, work in pairs and spend about 35 to 40 minutes with each applicant. In a sense it's the applicant who interviews us as he or she usually has a lot of questions to ask about the work that'd be expected.

After studying the applications in much depth, the search committee short-lists two or three applicants and invites them to spend a couple of days on campus. At the University's expense, of course.

During the time they're on campus, the applicants get to meet all the faculty and research students. They present their research, they're entertained by faculty, and then spend some time with the Dean.

Then everyone fills in an evaluation sheet, which includes questions on each applicant's personality and cultural fit. The search committee analyses the evaluations, ranks the three applicants and chooses the one who has the highest rank.

2nd recruiter

I manage a department store in the centre of London. We've got a permanent, full-time staff of 70 plus 40 or so part-timers who come in at weekends, during the tourist season and just before Christmas.

We recruit our sales assistants and cashiers mainly through adverts in the local paper – the *Evening News* or the *Evening Standard*, for example. We generally wait until there are at least three or four vacancies before placing an ad and, as a rule, we get between 100 and 200 applications.

For permanent positions we prefer to take people with some store experience, although this isn't absolutely essential; experience in selling or demonstrating products might be equally as valid. As far as qualifications are concerned, a school-leaving certificate is normally required, and some knowledge of foreign languages is a definite advantage.

On the basis of the written application we reject about two-thirds of the applicants. We invite the others to the store where our supervisors then show them around the various departments and answer any questions they may have. We then sit them down and ask them to take a short paper-and-pencil-test which is designed to reveal their speed and accuracy in solving problems, making simple calculations and using language correctly. While they are doing this our supervisors make a written note of each applicant's physical presentation – the way she's dressed, her physical appearance – and that's about it for the initial contact.

We'll then short-list about three times as many applicants as we have vacancies, and interview each of them individually. Actually, it's the store's personnel manager who interviews; I only get to meet them after the final selection has been made and they've started work.

3rd recruiter

I'm in charge of human resources for a major publishing house. We publish many of the world's leading titles for corporate decision-makers in the fields of business strategy, international investment, and global marketing.

Our recruitment methods depend very much on the kinds of vacancies we have. At the moment, for example, we're in the process of launching a number of important new titles, which has created six vacancies for high-calibre advertising sales executives. We're looking for articulate and motivated people who can deal effectively on the telephone with prospective advertisers.

For these positions we decided to place a number of advertisements in the national press, under the media and marketing section, giving details of the job and the profile we're seeking. We received about 130 applications, many of which were unsuitable because either the applicants didn't have the necessary experience in advertising sales or the presentation of his or her CV simply wasn't up to scratch; spelling mistakes, typing errors, badly organised cover letters, that kind of thing. We tend to feel that this is a reflection of the person's lack of appropriate communication skills and professionalism and, as a result, we rejected all those which weren't absolutely impeccable.

Out of the initial batch we invited 20 to come along for an interview, part of which was based on a simulation exercise. We actually had the candidates ring up a prospective customer (actually, the prospective customer was our deputy sales director) and try to sell her advertising space. We recorded the whole conversation on cassette, and analysed it later on. We also asked each applicant to draft a short business letter to a prospective customer.

We're still in the process of sorting through the evaluations we've made, but in view of the quality of some of the applicants, I don't think we'll have much trouble filling these vacancies. I'm hoping to interview the short-listed applicants within the next couple of weeks and will be looking in particular at their level of motivation.

2.2.E

	1st recruiter	2nd recruiter	3rd recruiter
1 Recruiter's position	Chairmain of Management Department	Store manager	Human Resources Manager
2 Organisation	Large State University	Department store in London	Major publishing house
3 Position(s) discussed	Professors	Sales assistants and cashiers	Advertising sales executives
4 Recruiting sources	Internal posting and management journals and reviews	Advertisements in local newspapers	Classified advertisments in national press
5 Typical response level	30–40	100–200	130
6 Screening criteria	Appropriate background	• relevant experience (store, sales, demonstrating) • school-leaving certificate	• relevant experience • presentation of written application
7 People encountered during 1st interview	Pairs of department faculty	Supervisors	Deputy Sales Director (on telephone)
8 People encountered during 2nd interview	• All faculty and research students • Dean	Personnnel Manager	Human Resources Manager
9 Tests	Presentation of research	Paper and pencil test for speed and accuracy	Sales simulation
10 Other criteria mentioned	Personality and cultural fit	Physical presentation	Level of motivation

2.2.F

1 d	2 o	3 c	4 p	5 l	6 b	7 g	8 m	9 k
10 e	11 h	12 n	13 a	14 f	15 i	16 j	17 q	18 r.

2.2.G

Alternative procedure for case study (variations are possible)

1 Each St reads case out of class and prepares 3 questions regarding content of case.
2 Each St reads designates another and tests his/her understanding of case by asking 1 question.
3 T asks for 4 volunteers to play the role of the 4 applicants. Set them aside and ask them to prepare their interview. This means anticipating the questions which might be asked and formulating some questions which they might ask the interviewer.
4 Divide others into 4 groups (A, B, C, D) and assign 1 applicant to each group. A, B, C, and D must imagine they are Jacques Bernard, and study the information on the short-listed applicants. A, B, C and D then prepare interviews.
5 Group A interviews Derek Hamper in front of the rest of the class. T should impose time limit.
6 After interview, T asks class if there are any other questions which should be asked.
7 Repeat exercise for groups B, C and D and other 3 applicants.
8 Analysis of interviews:
   a language correction
   b content; to what extent did interviewers discover whether applicants have required skills and track record?
9 Sts go through applicants one by one and evaluate each applicant's strengths and weaknesses. Should any of them be eliminated immediately? Are there any further elements you would wish to obtain before making an appointment?
10 Sts vote for each applicant (each St may vote for more than 1 applicant). Congratulate the successful applicant. Analyse the results (wide discrepancy, close-run contest, etc.).

UNIT 3

3.1.B

1 Four of the items were chosen by all three categories of staff; self-development and improvement is considered more important than chances for promotion; secretaries need acknowledgement/praise.

3 Programmes designed to increase staff motivation should concentrate on those items which are perceived as motivating.

3.1.C

1 membership	**2** turnover	**3** standard of living	**4** subcontractor
5 deadlines	**6** redundancies	**7** shift	**8** output
9 subsidised	**10** pension	**11** boredom	**12** fulfilment.

3.1.D

Motivating employees (tapescript)

1st manager

I work for a subsidiary of the Goodyear tyre manufacturing giant in Sydney, Australia. A few years ago, the factory was plagued by absenteeism so that at times our production lines were running at only 74% of capacity. The cost in terms of lost production and non-respect of delivery times was enormous and we realised that something drastic had to be done quickly. Of course, absenteeism isn't peculiar to our company; it's rife throughout Australian industry. It seems to be associated with affluence and the really superb climate so that workers can actually afford to take the occasional day off and go down to the beach even if it means losing a day's pay. If they *do* need to make up any shortfall in their pay packet they can always work a little bit of overtime.

Another thing is that workers in Australia are told exactly how many sick days they're allowed, which of course encourages them to take the maximum number, regardless of whether they're sick or not. Of course, boredom and monotony are also important factors but less so than the reasons I've just mentioned.

Anyway, the company decided to tackle the problem by rewarding good workers rather than punishing the bad ones. We sent a letter, hand delivered, to each of the worker's wives explaining that if their husband went to work regularly he would qualify for a prize, such as a diamond ring or a wrist watch. He wouldn't automatically get the prize, of course; each worker was put into a group and would only qualify for the prize if all the members of his group attended work regularly. At the end of the month, those groups who qualified were put into a draw. At the end of the third month, the groups which still qualified were put into a second draw for a colour TV set.

The results of the campaign were very impressive – in the short-term, at any rate. In the first few weeks we managed to cut the number of working days lost from 613 to 556 per week and within a couple of months attendance had improved by about 9.6%, though this fell back somewhat when the campaign ended.

As far as job boredom goes, the company has introduced a number of activities such as lunchtime concerts to keep the men's minds off their monotonous work. The results seem fairly encouraging though we still have some way to go if we are to achieve our target of running at 95% of our capacity.

2nd Manager

I'm Dean of a business school and the problem we had to tackle was how to get our professors more involved in the school. Many of them were, in my opinion, devoting too much of their time and energy to activities which were not directly benefiting the school. Some of them were giving classes in other schools, others were operating as part-time consultants. Some even had their own businesses in things like fashion design, import/export and market research. Many of them just came in to give their lessons and would then disappear for the rest of the day, although they were actually being paid full-time. I suppose their main motivation here was financial, though some genuinely needed something more challenging than the school was offering.

So the first thing I did when I became Dean was to insist on professors devoting their working hours exclusively to the school. If they want to work elsewhere they may do so, of course, but in their own time – in the evening or at weekends, for example. Or they can choose to work here part-time, and be paid pro rata. What they do for the rest of week is their own concern.

Secondly, I set up an annual commission to evaluate each professor's work. At the beginning of the year each professor has to draw up a list of his or her activities for the coming year; the number of classes he or she expects to give, research projects he or she'll be working on, publications, canvassing, development of new programmes, participation in symposiums, continuing education programmes he or she'll be studying on, and so on and so forth. At the end of the year the commission sees to what extent each professor's objectives have been met, and evaluates his work accordingly, both from a quantitative and a qualitative point of view.

I, myself, don't sit on the commission. The members of the commission are the professors themselves – some appointed by me, some elected by their peers – and it's they who send me a report on each professor, and this report forms the basis of any future decisions regarding raises and promotions.

The system met with a certain amount of resistance initially as some professors felt like Big Brother was watching them all the time. We also had some teething troubles, especially over the criteria for evaluating their performance. But I think we've now ironed out most of the problems and are beginning to transform the school from a small provincial teaching establishment to an internationally recognised institution with a strong research ethic, a highly committed team and a growing presence in the media and business reviews.

3rd Manager

I'm head of Human Resources for a car components manufacturer and the problem we were having a while back was high staff turnover. It affected us at all levels but especially among our junior and middle managers. At one point it was getting so bad that we had to replace 15 of our managers in the space of six months. Anyway, we decided to systematically interview everyone as soon as they handed in their notice so that we would get a clearer idea of why they were leaving us. It's amazing how much people will reveal in this kind of interview when they know they've got nothing to lose; they can be totally honest without worrying about the consequences.

What emerged from these interviews was that our people, whatever their position in the company, felt they weren't being trusted, It was a kind of vicious circle; the company doesn't trust the employees, so the employees don't trust the company to reward their talent and effort. So either they reduce their commitment by working less hard, or they quit.

We therefore decided to develop an atmosphere of mutual trust between top executives and employees, and I don't just mean managers but shop-floor workers as well. We started giving more authority to all employees by letting them have a greater voice in decisions. We figured that anyone who is likely to be affected by a particular decision ought to have the feeling that people want to know how he or she feels. In some cases it's enough to provide employees with a letter box so that they can make their feelings known, either anonymously or not. In other cases employee representatives are allowed to sit in on and actively participate in management meetings. Executives are encouraged to push responsibility down the ladder and delegate more to their immediate subordinates.

We've also tried to develop a stronger team spirit in the company by organising a weekly social evening in the bar, where employees at all levels can come and drink and dance and, hopefully, learn to trust each other a little more.

The change in attitude among employees is almost palpable. Productivity's up and staff turnover at all levels is down by as much as 10%.

3.1.D

	1st Manager	**2nd Manager**	**3rd Manager**
ORGANISATION	*Subsidiary of Goodyear*	*Business school*	*Manufacturer of car components*
CATEGORY OF EMPLOYEES CONCERNED	Production line workers	Professors	All levels, especially junior and middle managers
PROBLEM	Absenteeism	Lack of involvement	High staff turnover
CAUSE(S) OF PROBLEM	• affluence • climate • workers know their rights • boredom and monotony	• financial • school not challenging enough	• employees not trusted
STRATEGIES EMPLOYED	• rewarding good workers by putting them in prize draw • lunchtime concerts	• devote working hours to school • commission to evaluate professors	• give everyone greater voice in decisions • develop team spirit through social activities
RESULTS	• in short-term: cut in working days lost • attendance up by 9.6% • slight reversal of trend after campaign ended	• some problems but 'productivity' increasing/improving	• productivity up • staff turnover down by 10%

Suggested answers

1st manager

1   The wives would put pressure on their husbands to go to work. Working-class wives often handle the family budget.
2   Group pressure is a strong motivating force.
3   Appropriate in the short-term, as the figures show. However, success may be limited to short-term benefits only if workers have developed a strong group identity which can be harnessed to define group targets and group responsibilities.

2nd manager

1   Loss of contact with companies (the 'real' world); loss of income; presence does not mean productivity.
2   Advantages: effort and good results are acknowledged and rewarded; the very act of defining objectives is motivating. Disadvantages: the Big Brother syndrome; the difficulty in measuring work qualitatively.

3rd manager

1   The person leaving can afford to be frank and honest as he or she has nothing to lose, However, he or she may bear a grudge against somebody and take revenge. Information on work methods, personalities, abuses of power, etc.
2   Participating in potentially dangerous activities, for example, having to fall off a wall into the arms of trustworthy colleagues; complete openness.

3.1.E

Suggested answers

a   Is there a career structure? Why was there such a big increase in union membership recently? What changes (technical, structural) do you foresee if you win this contract?
b   Failure to adapt to a changing environment; pay not linked to performance therefore not motivating; old-fashioned, conservative corporate structure in a high-tech sector.
c   Recruit older workers with a stronger work ethic; organise activities to help communication and build a corporate identity; link pay to performance and eliminate automatic annual increments.

3.2.B

1   US personnel cope rather badly; a high proportion are recalled or dismissed due to poor performance. Japanese companies report a much lower failure rate for their personnel.
2   $200,00 to maintain a US family overseas; operations disrupted (loss of contracts, loss of confidence, loss of opportunities); valuable human asset lost (high cost of replacing him/her; even non-failure may not mean success (working to less than full capacity).
3   Before departure: thorough selection, followed by training in culture, customs, language and ways of doing business.
    During assignment: a mentor, contact with head office, reassurance about future.
    After completion: good chance of promotion ('integral step in career plan').
4   In most cases, none. In some cases there is an informational briefing but this is inadequate.
5   Short-stay technicians: survival skills eg cultural awareness.
    Long-term expatriates: effectiveness skills eg learning to adjust and to appreciate the foreign culture.
    Foreign nationals coming to the US: needs vary, according to country of origin.

3.2.E

Suggested answers

By far the biggest gap between highest and lowest paid executives is in Hong Kong. This gap indicates the importance of money as a motivator. The opposite is true of Norway.

**Company focus:
People in BP**

1   A 'flatter organisation' is relatively decentralised with few levels in its hierarchy and greater delegation of authority to middle managers.
2   Opportunity 2000 is a campaign to improve the ratio of women to men in the UK workforce.
3   BP provides day-care facilities for children where practicable (nurseries, childcare centres, replacement care); employees are encouraged to become shareholders in BP; BP encourages disabled people with a suitable qualification to work there; BP is striving to lead the way in HSE.
    Advantages for BP: becoming a shareholder means that the employee is more involved in the company and has a financial interest in its success. Offering childcare facilities means that there is less likelihood of absenteesim and lateness, extended maternity or paternity leave becomes less of a necessity, and young parents develop a stronger loyalty to the company. Disabled employees are likely to be more loyal than others due to their restricted mobility. Furthermore, the company's image is greatly enhanced. A good HSE performance is essential for the company's image and for its future efficiency and profitability.

Extension

This extract provides many discussion opportunities. For example, you could discuss to what extent corporations such as BP reflect the values of those societies in which they operate, and to what extent they shape them. Will women ever achieve perfectly equal status with men in the workplace? What are the barriers to equality in different societies? To what extent do companies have a commitment to the community in which they operate? Is this commitment a two-way process?

UNIT 4

4.1.C

1 Convenience goods: toothpaste; razor blades
Convenience services: dry cleaner; hairdresser (could also be considered as a shopping service, depending on how much effort the consumer is prepared to make to purchase the service)
Shopping goods: washing machine; bed
Shopping services: interior decorator; accountant
Speciality goods: an Aston Martin; Savile Row suit; Breitling watch
Speciality services: medical specialist; a meal at Maxim's
Expense items: paper clips; janitorial services; small components
Capital items: truck; robot

2 *Suggested answers*
soap; washing up liquid; shoelaces; phone call; taxi; stamp; freezer; car; vet; university; Rolls Royce; Van Gogh painting; Arianne; dog cemetery; stapler; staples; bulldozer; fax.

4 **a** negative publicity **b** reseller support **c** reseller support **d** positive publicity **e** sales promotion.

5 Other examples of white goods are: coffee maker, food mixer, tumble dryer, washing machine, dishwasher, microwave oven, iron, cooker. Other examples of brown goods are: tape recorder, VCR, CD player, cine camera, camescope.

6 Other examples of retail outlets are: mail order catalogue, open-air market, covered market, grocer's, greengrocer's, newsagent's, tobacconist's, off licence, department store, boutique, showroom, dealer, trade fair, chemist, duty-free shop, vending machine, mobile shop, High Street store, specialised store, supermarket, cash and carry.

4.1.D

1 k	**2** l	**3** h	**4** p	**5** a	**6** b	**7** f	**8** c	**9** o
10 m	**11** g	**12** i	**13** e	**14** n	**15** j	**16** d.		

4.2.A

Suggested answers
Silky Soft is the market leader with 23.4% of the market share; the four main products control over 70% of the market; Wild Girl is losing ground to its main rival, Vo-gel; the gap is widening between Vo-gel and Wild Girl; Silky Soft's promotion budget was much lower in 1992 than 1991; in 1992, Silky Soft sales in Asia outstripped sales in Europe; by the late 1990s, South America will be Silky Soft's main market; the large promotion budget in 1991 may have been for the launch of Silky Soft in South America.

4.2.B

1 from; to
2 suffered/saw/witnessed/experienced; drop/fall/decline/decrease
3 stable/unchanged/steady
4 enjoyed/saw/recorded
5 radically/sharply/drastically/substantially/dramatically/significantly
6 entered; took/captured/gained/conquered
7 (by)
8 regularly/steadily/seriously; sharply
9 quarter
10 fluctuation
11 approximately/roughly/about/around.

4.3.A

Making proposals and counter-proposals	**Reformulating information**
2 10	18 20
Expressing opinions	**Inviting a concession**
3 15	6 16
Disagreeing	**Asking for clarification**
4 8	1 11
Querying	**Asking for further information**
19 7	13 17
Offering advice	**Agreeing**
5 12	9 14

4.3.C

Procedure for role play
1 Sts read case study, preferably out of class.
2 T answers any questions which may arise. T asks a St to summarise case
3 In pairs, Sts each choose a role and carry out the negotiation (15 minutes max).
4 After negotiation, each pair feeds back to the class the agreement reached. T should note variables on board to compare results, especially the introduction of new variables, eg. Who bears transport costs? Which port of entry? Opening the Coventry plant for prospective purchasers of Excalibur? Negotiating a maintenance contract.
5 Who obtained the most favourable conditions? Who feels satisfied or unsatisfied with the outcome? Who respected the negotiation guidelines?

4.3.D

1 | 1 break into | 2 launching | 3 promoting | 4 carving |
   |---|---|---|---|
   | 5 accomplish | 6 struck | 7 quoted | 8 placed |
   | 9 reap | 10 infringing. | | |

2 | 1 accomplishment | 2 quotation | 3 infringement | 4 promotion |
   |---|---|---|---|
   | 5 presentation | 6 persuasion | 7 purchase | 8 inducement |
   | 9 knowledge | 10 exhibition | 11 display | 12 distribution |
   | 13 specialisation | 14 sample | 15 sale | 16 coverage |
   | 17 analysis | 18 relationship | 19 rise | 20 suggestion. |

UNIT 5

5.1.C

1 | 1 r | 2 j | 3 u | 4 h | 5 e | 6 i | 7 b | 8 q | 9 l |
   |---|---|---|---|---|---|---|---|---|
   | 10 t | 11 v | 12 f | 13 a | 14 n | 15 s | 16 o | 17 p | 18 c |
   | 19 m | 20 k | 21 d | 22 g. | | | | | |

2 *Suggested answers:*
print media	b, e, g, h, i, j , k, l, n, p, q, r, t, u
broadcasting media	a, f, s
others	b, c, d, m, o, v

5.1.E

How an advertising budget is established (tapescript)
Today, we're going to talk about four basic methods for establishing an advertising budget. Let's quickly list them on the board. They are:

- the affordable method
- the percentage of sales method
- the competitive parity method and, finally
- the objective and task method.

Now these are the most popular methods for establishing an advertising budget, but as we shall see, they are not all very logical. Let's begin by having a look at the strengths and weaknesses of each method.

First of all, the affordable method. We will ask for everything the company can afford to give us; if the company had a good year last year, they'll give us a lot; if not, they'll give us a little, or perhaps even nothing at all.

The two main weaknesses of this method are that, firstly, it leads to a *fluctuating advertising budget* over time. And secondly, it makes *long-term planning difficult.* How can we expect our marketing people to come up with an advertising strategy when they don't know from one year to the next how much money they'll have to play with? The smaller the organisation, the more likely it is to use this method because small organisations don't plan anyway. It's not that they shouldn't, it's that they don't. The main advantage of the affordable method is that the company only spends what it can afford; there's no danger of it overspending. Is everybody clear about the affordable method? Any questions? Right.

The second method we're going to look at today is the percentage of sales method. The percentage of sales method is the most popular method. The company's advertising budget is based on the preceding year's sales for the product or products in question.

Now, what are the weaknesses of this method? Well, firstly there's a complete absence of theory to justify this method. No model has ever been devised to support it. Secondly, this method leads to circular reasoning; in other words, according to this method, sales are causing advertising rather than the reverse, advertising causing sales. Our advertising shouldn't be a function of what happened in the past but should contribute to sales in the future. That's what we mean by circular reasoning.

A third drawback is that this method sets up a vicious circle; if we had a bad year last year, we'll spend less on advertising this year and therefore increase our chances of having another bad year. In other words, the percentage of sales method may prohibit the use of counter-cyclical advertising strategies. OK. Let me explain what we mean by counter-cyclical advertising strategies. A counter-cyclical advertising strategy means that if sales were down last year we may help to remedy the situation by proper, creative advertising, which may mean spending a correspondingly larger amount than last year, not a smaller amount. Consequently, we may continue to spiral downward.

A fourth weakness of the method is this: what percentage of last year's sales should we pick as a reference point? Should it be 1%, 3% or 4.5%? Should it be the same for all the company's brands? Is there such a thing as a logical fixed percentage? In actual fact, those companies which use this method tend to have a fixed percentage for all their products and this really doesn't make sense, does it, because apart from the fact that this fixed percentage is not logical but arbitrary, the brands which we want to advertise may be in very different stages of evolution. For example, some brands are in the introduction stage of the product life cycle and may require hefty advertising budgets, while others are in the maturity stage. Some brands have been successful, others unsuccessful. There are so many factors that it's crazy to come up with *one* fixed percentage, never mind deciding what that percentage should be.

There are, however, a few positive things to say about the percentage of sales method. It's true, for example, that the company won't get into trouble by overspending; it will only spend what it can afford to spend. Also, this method does encourage management to look at the relationships between advertising costs, selling prices and profits per unit, and this *analysis* of relationship can be very valuable. A third advantage is that this method, when followed by a lot of companies, may encourage competitive stability, especially when the fixed percentage that companies pick is roughly the same. Competitive stability means that there are no advertising wars and this can be good for the individual firms.

Now let's talk now about the third method; the competitive parity method. We find out what our competitors are spending and we attempt to match what they spend. We'd probably look at what four or five of our major competitors spent last year and calculate the average of what they spend, then we'll say 'That's what we'll spend next year on our advertising'.

Now, what's the rationale behind this method? Well, firstly, our competitors' expenditure on advertising ought to represent the collective wisdom of the industry. And secondly, because we do spend about the same amount of money as our competitors, this ought to prevent advertising wars.

The problem is that these two assumptions don't hold water. There's no reason to assume that our competitors represent any wisdom at all; they may be as much in the dark as we are. Who's to say they're smarter than we are, that their techniques are more sophisticated? And as far as preventing advertising wars, well that's nonsense as well because if any of our competitors want to spend more on advertising this year they'll do it.

The last method is known as the objective and task method. First of all, let's see what it is. If we can establish what our advertising objectives are, we ought to be able to figure out what we need to do in order to reach those objectives.

So, for this to work, we have to be able to do the following: firstly we have to define our advertising objectives as specifically as possible. For example, what is the target market and what do we want our ad to do? Do we want it to inform, to change attitudes, do we want it to reinforce existing attitudes, to encourage buying behaviour. . .? Whatever it is, it must be specified. Then we can go to the second step, which is, 'What specific tasks have to be performed to achieve these objectives?'. For example, if we choose as an advertising objective 'imparting knowledge', in other words we want to teach our target market something new, what do we have to do to get that across? We have to create a theme, a system, whereby we know which media we're going to position our ads in. We have to have our whole creative staff working on the internal characteristics of the ad. And all those activities cost money.

So the final step is to estimate the costs of each task and just add them up. Now this may sound easy on paper. It's entirely consistent with marketing theory which says you must establish your general objectives first, learn about the target market, do your segmentation, do your positioning, learn about the competition, then take the whole wealth of information, then, *then,* establish specific marketing objectives and then advertising objectives. It is very much consistent with that.

However, it is the most difficult method to implement and requires a great deal of rigour in order to carry it out successfully.

5.1.E

Method	Budget based on	Strengths	Weaknesses
1 Affordable	Whatever company can afford	Can't overspend	Fluctuating advertising budget; long-term planning difficulties
2 Percentage of sales	Percentage of last year's sales	• ditto • encourages analysis of relationship between costs, prices and profits per unit • encourages competitive stability	• no theory • circular reasoning (sales causes advertising) • vicious circle • no logical percentage
3 Competitive parity	Average of whatever competitors spend	• represents collective wisdom? • prevents advertising wars?	• both assumptions illogical • 'average' doesn't take into account discrepancies
4 Objective and task	Costing tasks needed to reach objectives	Entirely consistent with marketing theory	Difficult to implement

    1 Small businesses because they don't usually plan.
    2 Inform; change attitudes; reinforce existing attitudes; encourage buying behaviour.

5.2.A

Medium	Advantages	Disadvantages
Newspaper	• broad reach • advertising permanence • all-year-round readership • geographical selectivity and flexibility	• limited colour availability with variable quality • little demographic selectivity
Television	• appeal to senses of sight and sound • frequent messages • broad target	• high cost • short-lived message • VCR viewers skip advertising
Direct mail	• can target very specific prospects • ability to saturate specific area • flexible format and style	• consumer resistance • high cost per exposure
Radio	• low cost • large potential audiences • specific targets	• listeners don't listen • no visual possibilities
Magazines	• permanence of message • read by many • good quality reproduction • great selectivity	• high costs • long preparation time

Extension
There are many ways in which the theme of the advertising media may be developed.
Here are some ideas:
    1 Discussions, based on the advertising media in the students' home countries. For example, how well developed is direct mail or telephone selling? How do people react to it? How do you, personally, react?

2 Cultural input, for example, a mini-lecture on the press in Britain (the main dailies and Sundays, their circulation and readership, their political allegiance, who reads them, etc). This could be followed up with an activity based on students reading a cross section of British newspapers and commenting on them (eg comparison of layout, style, content, advertising, what all this tells us about the British and British mentalities, how these differ from the students' compatriots, etc). A similar activity might be carried out for any of the other media and any other English-speaking country.

5.3.A

Suggested answers
Television and newspapers attract the biggest budgets; cinema advertising is dominated by advertising for tobacco and alcohol (legislation restricts this advertising in many other media); automobiles is the biggest spending industry and Renault the biggest spending company; two prestigious cosmetics companies advertise heavily in magazines (quality image, fine targeting); less prestigious cosmetics and hygiene products are advertised heavily on television; some companies spread their advertising budget over a wide variety of media while others concentrate their efforts on one medium.

5.3.B

Suggested answers
During the summer, people spend more time outside; people spend Christmas indoors with their family; after a heavy Christmas meal people don't want to move much; parents put their children to bed around 8pm and can't watch television until later on.

5.3.C

1 1 l	**2** a	**3** d	**4** o	**5** u	**6** y	**7** k	**8** b	**9** t
10 i	**11** j	**12** f	**13** w	**14** q	**15** g	**16** s	**17** e	**18** c
19 v	**20** h	**21** r	**22** x	**23** p	**24** n	**25** m.		

3 1 the horse-racing press
   2 the Italian wine market
   3 basketball shoes
   4 advertising support
   5 yoghurt pots.

UNIT 6

6.1.A

1 F   **2** T   **3** F   **4** F   **5** T   **6** F.

6.1.B

Suggested answers
1 Retailers grouping together to negotiate purchases has meant that producers have had to reduce their sales force.
2 The consequence of retailers employing highly-trained purchasers is that producers have had to employ highly-trained salesmen.
3 Retailers have developed their own generic brands, which has led to producers having to compete with them.
4 Due to the development of sophisticated logistics by retailers, producers now deal with fewer delivery points.
5 Products need to sell themselves because of the development of self-service.
6 Failure to keep pace with competition has brought about a reduction in the number of retail outlets.
7 The growing importance of merchandising is a result of customers having direct contact with products.
8 The spread of the automobile has enabled retailers to locate on outskirts of town.

6.1.C

1 display racks	**2** shelf space	**3** retail chains
4 cash desk	**5** trolley	**6** DIY
7 central purchasing offices	**8** signposting; entrance	**9** counter.

6.1.D

The layout of a supermarket (tapescript)
As in most supermarkets nowadays, the check-out desks are situated on the left-hand side of the entrance because customers tend to move down the aisles in an anti-clockwise direction.

The customer enters the supermarket and passes through the fresh fruit and vegetable area where she can select what ever she wants and then weigh the produce on the electronic scales. These are situated just opposite the emergency exit. The scales not only weigh, but price the product automatically, and we've found that this is the fastest and cheapest way of serving customers.

On the right-hand side of the aisle after the emergency exit, there's a self-service counter for cooked meats and poultry. The cheese counter is situated at right-angles to this so that it can be clearly seen as the customer walks down the aisle. We've got a good range of British and Continental cheeses which the customer can have cut fresh from the block.

Just in front of the cheese counter, there's a small floating island of pre-packaged sausage and salamis.

Turning left at the cheese counter, the customer passes by two rows of cleaning products, such as washing-up liquid, soap powder, detergent, furniture polish and floor wax, that kind of thing, then there are four rows for wines, spirits, beer and soft drinks, in that order. These are high-margin products so we've placed them in a very prominent position which every customer has to pass by.

Opposite the drinks department, there's the fish counter which sells a wide range of fresh fish and seafood. This is followed by a special section for fruit juice, UHT milk and mineral water which are all rather bulky, fast-moving products and which therefore require a special area next to the stockroom in order to simplify restocking the shelves.

Opposite that, and backing onto the row of soft drinks, there's one row for toilet paper then one row for babies' nappies. Then, as you can see, there are two rows for canned goods, such as canned fruit, canned vegetables and canned fish, then one row of savoury snacks, you know, crisps, peanuts, salty crackers and so on.

Following on from that, there's one row for flour, rice and pasta followed by a row of health food products, like salt-free biscuits, high-fibre cereals, vitamins and minerals and things to make you live longer if you can afford to pay the price.

Moving on down the aisle, you've got one row for tea and coffee followed by one row of breakfast cereals and children's snacks, including bars of chocolate and packets of sweets.

The next row is given over to jam, marmalade and honey and that's followed by two rows of biscuits. After that, there's one row of pet food, followed by two rows for cooking oils and condiments. The last two rows are for dairy produce such as butter, cheese, margarine and eggs.

On the right-hand side of the aisle, opposite the biscuits, there's the meat counter with two butchers serving full-time, and next to that, right in the corner there's a cooked-meat counter with one sales assistant.

Turning left at the end of the aisle, there are two counters, the one on the left being for frozen food, the one on the right is for dairy produce, such as fresh milk, cream, yogurts, and milk-based desserts.

This is followed by two more frozen-food counters, the one on the left being for pizzas, fish fingers and beef burgers, the right-hand one is for ice-creams and frozen desserts.

Turning left, then, at the emergency exit, you've got the administration offices on your right followed by the sugar section. At right-angles to that, there's the bread and cakes counter, with a wide range of products.

On the other side of the aisle there are eight rows given over to seasonal products such as toys and chocolates at Christmas, or bulbs and seeds in the Spring.

Following on from that, there's one row for small electrical items such as batteries, light bulbs and plugs, then two rows of DIY material and two rows for soaps and cosmetics.

The last five rows are given over to hardware (you know, saucepans, frying pans, pressure cookers, that sort of thing), crockery (cups, plates, saucers and glasses), cutlery, and two rows of electrical goods such as toasters, hairdriers, coffee-makers, clocks and electric shavers.

Back-to-back with the fruit and vegetable counter there's the stationery department where we stock a fairly wide selection of newspapers and magazines, as well as pens, paper and envelopes.

The head cashier's office is on the right of the stationery department, and she keeps an eye on the ten check-out desks in front of her. Her permanent presence is an effective control against check-out desk irregularities.

The layout of the supermarket is of paramount importance in optimising sales. As you can see, we've spread out the location of the basic foodstuffs such as sugar, flour, oil, pasta, milk and bread into various parts of the supermarket so that the consumer has to visit all four corners of the store to get everything she needs, Hopefully, she'll do some impulse shopping on the way.

On average the consumer spends around 20 minutes in the supermarket, which is typical for a store of this size. It's vital that she spends a very limited amount of time purchasing the basic products, and rather more time impulse shopping. In order to encourage this behaviour, we try to keep the traffic moving by having wide, well-lit, well sign-posted aisles.

We also have a number of gondolas at the intersection of two aisles for displays and demonstrations, and of course there are the usual display racks at the check-out desks for small, high-margin articles such as chewing gum and razor blades.

One final point of interest is the use of children's trolleys which, we've noticed, has boosted sales for things like biscuits and sweets.

1

1 electronic scales	**2** cooked meats and poultry	**3** sausage and salamis
4 wines	**5** spirits	**6** beer
7 soft drinks	**8** fish counter	**9** babies' nappies
10 canned goods	**11** canned goods	**12** health food
13 cereals and children's snacks	**14** biscuits	**15** biscuits
16 pet food	**17** dairy produce	**18** dairy produce
19 cooked meat	**20** frozen food	**21** frozen food
22 frozen food	**23** sugar	**24** bread and cakes
25 small electrical items	**26** DIY	**27** DIY
28 electrical goods	**29** electrical goods	**30** stationery.

2 Spreading out of basic products; well-lit, well-signposted aisles; display racks; floating isles; children's trolleys.
Bulky and fast-moving items are given a special area next to the stockroom.
Head cashier's office located next to check-out desks.

3 *Suggested answers*
- polish, wax, bleach, sponges
- seafood (mussels, shrimps, prawns, oysters) and fish (cod, hake, skate, salmon)
- crisps, peanuts, cashew nuts, crackers
- cream, yoghurt, milk, eggs, cheese
- cups, plates, saucers, mugs.

6.3.A

Warehouse clubs (tapescript)
Over the past few years we've seen an interesting trend developing in American retailing, namely the warehouse club, or cash-and-carry store. Basically, these are enormous stores which offer their members absolute rock-bottom prices on a range of products such as food and household appliances. Prices are typically somewhere between 20% and 40% lower than you'd find in the local supermarket. There are probably around 30 of these warehouse clubs in the US. You'll find them in most of the main towns and their sales this year are expected to reach around $7 billion.

They rely on a very rapid turnover of inventory, usually between 15 to 18 times a year, and their gross profit margin is 10%. You have to be a member to buy at one of these clubs, which means paying a $25 annual membership fee. About half of the clubs' sales are to business customers – small shops, restaurants, local factories, that kind of thing.

There are many reasons why these warehouse clubs are able to undercut their competitors to such an extent. Firstly, they offer no amenities, I mean these places are really like warehouses – grey walls, shelves going right up to the ceiling, virtually no sales assistants to give advice. And then, of course, they spend practically nothing on advertising; well, they don't really need to, I suppose. Also, they offer a very limited selection of products; they concentrate only on products that they can move quickly which means they've got less capital tied up in inventory.

Another big advantage they have is their size and the economies of scale which go with that. For example, their overheads are spread over greater sales, which keeps unit costs down. Similarly, their size means they can be tough in negotiating with suppliers so they get all the best buys. And, finally, because so many of their customers are business people, there's less likelihood of being paid with dud cheques.

In spite of all these advantages, though, warehouse clubs are not likely to radically transform American retailing. In fact, their effect has been only minimal because each warehouse club takes only a little away from its competitors, and as there are still relatively few clubs I don't think they'll seriously upset the present status quo – not for the time being anyway.

1 **a** Between 20% and 40%
   b About 30
   c $7 billion
   d 15 to 18 times a year
   e $25 per year
   f 10%
   g 50%.
2 no amenities; little advertising; less capital tied up in inventory; fixed costs spread over greater sales; customers less prone to writing bad cheques; clubs look for the best buys and are tough negotiators.
3 Very little impact because there are so few of them and they take only a little away from each competitor.

6.3.B

(Alternative adjectives are in brackets.)
1 fierce (cut-throat; harsh)
3 critical (key; major)
5 slender (slim; meagre)
7 first rate (admirable; splendid)
9 handy (practical)
11 destructive (harmful)
13 lax (slack).

2 slack (sluggish; languid)
4 colossal (gigantic; immense)
6 gratifying (satisfying; enjoyable)
8 burning (unyielding; irresistible)
10 conventional (orthodox)
12 reckless (rash)

6.3.C

1 distribution
3 appealing
5 growth; concentration
7 sales
9 produce
11 consumption
13 reduction
15 advertisement; commercial
17 discoveries; marketable
19 conquer

2 shortage
4 regulations
6 compete
8 alterations
10 sizeable
12 salespeople/salesmen/saleswomen
14 consumers; increasingly
16 disposable
18 economical
20 diversify.

6.3.D

A shopping mall (tapescript)

The first shopping malls grew up in the immediate post-war period as a response to the deep changes that were taking place in American society. For example, the early 50s saw the greatest spread of suburban life in America, with the middle classes moving out of the city into the suburbs. This was linked, of course, to the tremendous population explosion – the so-called 'baby boom' – and America's increasing affluence. The automobile became affordable by most people so that distances became indifferent. To meet the needs of this huge, affluent population who no longer had the traditional city centres to serve them, a new industry was created; the shopping centre, or mall, as it came to be known. At the same time, American culture went very private, from a communal culture centred around the town square, with the traditional European nineteenth century notions of urbanity, to a very private, very materialistic culture based on consumption.

One of the first mall designers was Victor Gruen, and his aim was to provide an identifying focus for suburbia. He saw the mall as an opportunity of giving suburbia a core, a definition. The hope was that the mall would grow into an urban centre, not merely devoted to retailing, and surrounded by cars, but that it would be joined by public facilities, museums, services, even educational facilities. Unfortunately, this didn't come to pass in the 1950s. The first shopping centres became exclusively dictated to by commercial criteria, and it was only in the 80s that mall designers began to incorporate non-commercial amenities.

Victor Gruen also saw the mall as a way of dealing with the car in a comprehensive way. The car had always been accommodated either by making wider streets or by making more parking places, or by demolishing buildings to make more parking lots. But usually the pedestrian was the loser in the conflict. So Gruen wanted to create a space where you'd be able to take the car but then forget about it and the mall would then be a space rather like the old public square.

This LA mall is a good example of a 1980s model, with a very wide range of facilities. For example, it has the largest indoor water park in the world, with 22 water slides and a wave machine which can generate waves up to six feet high. There are indoor and outdoor suntanning facilities. There's the 'Colorado River Rapids' ride; Fantasyland, with 25 rides and attractions including 'The Daring Drop of Doom'; the highest metal rollercoaster in the world, the 'Perilous Pendulum'. Then there's the deep-sea adventure area with four submarines, dolphins, sharks, alligators, penguins. And when you ride on the submarine you see these animals and many other forms and varieties of underwater wildlife.

The mall also has over 100 restaurants, 24 theatres, a zoo, an ice-skating rink, tennis courts, a chapel, an office tower housing dozens of lawyers, doctors, dentists and social workers, not to mention the mall's fifteen major department stores and over 500 other retail outlets. And all this under one roof! You really have to see it to believe it.

But despite the introduction of public facilities and services, the mall remains, first and foremost, a giant commercial venture, in fact one of the most powerful marketing mechanisms ever devised. The layout of the mall is designed in such a way as to maximise the chances of each individual shopper spending a maximum amount of money. It does this by transforming destination shoppers into impulse shoppers. For example, suppose you wanted to buy a pair of shoes for your six-year-old daughter. In marketing terms you'd be a 'destination shopper', in other words, a consumer who had come to the mall with a specific purchase in mind. Now, suppose you can't find exactly what you want at the first store you visit; you head off towards another shoe store but on the way you pass by several dozen other stores, cafés, ice-cream parlours, and what have you. By the time you arrive at the second shoe store there's a very good chance you will have bought something on the way which you hadn't originally planned to buy. In other words, you'd have been transformed from a 'destination shopper' into an 'impulse shopper'.

The design of the mall also owes a lot to Disneyland, which first introduced the idea of the 'theme environment', where complex reality is reduced to a number of easily understood themes. This idea has been taken up by almost every area of American existence ie shops, restaurants, tourist attractions and leisure facilities – they've all become theme environments so that now we travel in a circuit going from one theme environment to another without ever having to confront the realities of a city in between.

And this, of course, is another of the mall's main attractions. In the mall, you don't find the pickpockets, the pushers and the muggers that you'd find in most city centres. The mall is a relatively safe place. The parking lot is monitored by closed-circuit TV cameras, and there are plain-clothed and uniformed security guards who supervise the entire area. Any 'undesirable' elements are quickly moved on, and I don't only mean potential delinquents or hooligans, but homeless people, groups of adolescents and people whose behaviour may be bad for business.

In some ways the mall is a world within a world. We've created our own world by taking the outside and putting it inside. We've put the stores inside, and the trees and the animals, so that we can protect it and keep it clean and 'nice' all the time. And we've left all the rest, all the chaos we've created, out on the highway.

1 Mass middle class move from towns to suburbs; population explosion (baby boom); increasing affluence; automobile ownership; cultural shift from 'communal' to 'private'.
2 An identifying focus for suburbia, a core, a definition; an urban centre with a full range of facilities; a way of dealing with the automobile without penalising the pedestrian.

3 Water park; suntanning facilities; rides and attractions; deep-sea adventure area; restaurants; theatres; zoo; ice-skating rink; tennis courts; chapel; lawyers; doctors; dentists; social workers; department stores and other retail outlets.

4 By turning them from destination shoppers into impulse shoppers; by making them pass by a large number of stores before reaching their destination.

5 Safety for people and cars, thanks to very tight supervision by the security forces.

6 There is the 'Fantasyland' area; the mall successfully excludes 'undesirable' aspects of urban reality which might otherwise interfere with customers' happiness.

Company focus: Marketing at United Distillers

1 Geographical segmentation: Four geographical regions (Europe, North America, Asia-Pacific, international); certain brands are developed for certain geographical markets (eg White Horse Extra Fine, developed for the Japanese market).
Segmentation by quality and image: A broad range of products carefully positioned in a precisely defined sector (eg the top end of the de luxe sector, the premium gift market, the standard category); the price and choice of distribution outlet reflect the degree of prestige for each brand.

2 It enhances the prestigious image of the Old Parr brand (and of Scotch whisky overall) by its quality, its price and its distribution outlets.

3 Great importance – for example, ceramic bottles for the premium gift market; extensive research leading to new, more distinctive designs; a new design for one market; the upgrading of Cardhu's packaging to enhance its unique positioning.

4 As White Horse is the premium brand leader in Japan, Glen Elgin will benefit from the White Horse image.

5 The company not only produces spirits but also owns sales and marketing companies throughout the world and has joint ventures, notably with LVMH (wines, spirits, luxury goods).

6 The most important brand, the one which sets the image for other brands in the product range.

7 Its success can be measured by the strength of its brands; the four elements of the Marketing Mix work together in a consistent way to reinforce the image of each of its brands.

UNIT 7

7.1.B

1a Debt capital is money that the company has borrowed and which it must repay, with interest, at a later date. Equity capital is money raised through selling a share of ownership in the company. The company rewards its shareholders, whenever possible, by giving them a share of its profits in the form of dividends.

b Leasing is the loan of an item with an option to buy, whereas hire purchase is the purchase of an item – it belongs to the purchaser but may be redeemed if the purchaser defaults on the instalments.

c Both are transferable loans, but secured bonds are backed by collateral whereas debentures are not.

d Interest is the cost of borrowing money (or the reward for lending money) whereas dividends represent a share of the company's profits; if the company makes no profit, or decides to plough back all of its profits, it will not pay dividends and has no obligations to do so.

e Open-book credit is informal, short-term, interest-free credit which a supplier may offer a customer. Promissory notes are more formal in that each agreement is signed and the customer pays interest.

7.1.C

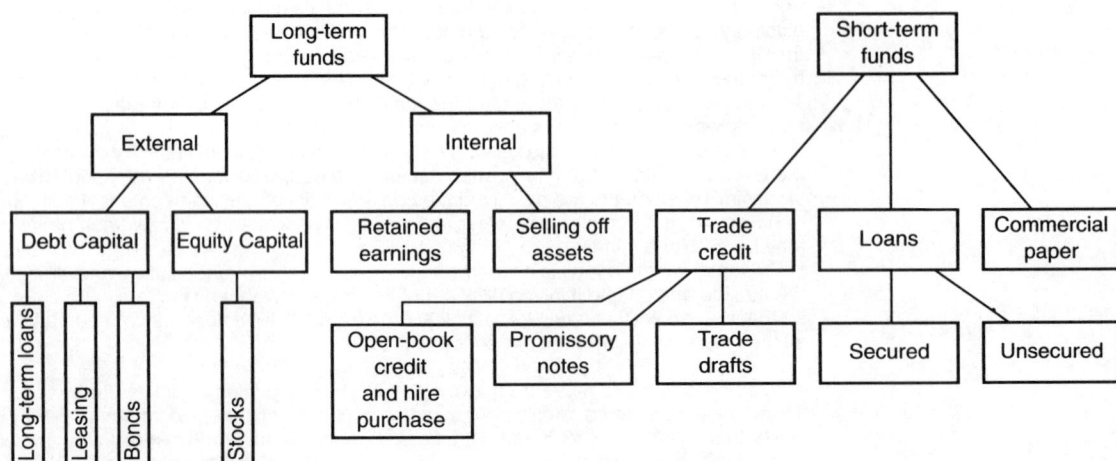

7.1.D

1 d	**2** r	**3** u	**4** c	**5** y	**6** e	**7** i	**8** h	**9** s
10 f	**11** p	**12** z	**13** o	**14** t	**15** v	**16** j	**17** g	**18** q
19 a	**20** k	**21** x	**22** l	**23** n	**24** b	**25** w	**26** m.	

7.1.E

Suggested answers

1 Free credit therefore extremely important for many businesses. However, suppliers may investigate customer's credit rating and limit size of credit accordingly.
2 Easier for risky customers to obtain credit; a means of obtaining more credit. However, capital plus interest must be repaid by a stipulated date; the supplier's bank acts as bill collector and generally has highly persuasive powers.
3 Can be used to obtain credit from overseas suppliers who might otherwise be reluctant to grant credit. However, the trade draft agreement may not grant credit for more than a few days.
4 Companies can usually obtain much bigger loans if they are backed by collateral. However, they risk having their assets seized if the loan is not repaid on time.
5 Useful for companies with good credit ratings and good earning power to raise funds. However, other companies may need to maintain a compensating balance at the bank, which may prove expensive.
6 Useful for large corporations with good credit ratings to raise loans with a payback period of between three and 270 days. Also, interest rates are fixed, which, in a time of rising interest rates, is beneficial to the borrower. However, commercial paper may not be used to finance long-term projects.
7 The repayment period may be very long indeed (up to 15 years in the US) but the interest rates are generally higher than for short-term loans, the risk of default being greater.
8 Leasing may be a good alternative for a company with a poor credit rating that has difficulty obtaining loans. It is particularly useful for companies whose assets are mostly large pieces of equipment eg airline companies, trucking companies. Furthermore, leasing often provides tax advantages. However, the cost may be relatively high.
9 Useful for borrowing large sums of money which would be difficult to obtain from a single source. By issuing bonds, the company is borrowing from several investors. However, the riskier the borrower, the higher the interest rate it must offer to attract investors. For example, junk bonds offer high interest but also high risk, and were used in the 1980s by corporate raiders as a way of financing takeovers.
10 An extremely important way of raising funds without having to pay interest. A company that sells stock may survive a few bad years by omitting dividends. However, stockholders may have a voice in management and the company thereby loses some control.

7.2.A

Company	Needs	Source(s) of funds
1 Computer manufacturer (annual earnings 1992: $3 billion)	to buy new plant and equipment	• retained earnings • bonds
2 Medium-sized car dealer	to buy 12 vehicles for immediate display in showroom (prime lending rate: 13%)	• short-term capital from bank
3 Small producer of kitchen furniture	to have enough ready cash to cover immediate expenses	• reduce accounts receivable • reduce inventory • trade credit
4 Small manufacturer	to purchase 10 industrial drills	• leasing
5 Large producer of ski-ing equipment with top credit-rating	to meet immediate expenses during off-season (prime lending rate: 18%)	• commercial paper • short-term bank loan
6 Overseas electronics wholesaler with unknown credit rating	to buy a large consignment of VCRs	• trade draft/trade acceptance
7 Clothes store with poor credit rating	to purchase stock for the summer season	• promissory notes
8 Major oil company	to build a 1,000 km pipeline from a newly discovered oil-field to the sea	• bonds • equity (common stock) • long-term bank loan
9 Leading chemical manufacturer	to finance acquisition of major competitor (forecast: two or three years before business takes off again)	• equity • long-term bank loan

7.2.B   **1** f   **2** e   **3** d   **4** g   **5** b.

7.2.C   *Suggested answers*
1 Banks have certainly benefited from the increasing use of credit cards (11 words).
2 Unfortunately, credit cards have encouraged some people to overspend (9 words).
3 Banks should impose stricter measures to protect families from becoming permanently indebted (12 words).
4 Western bankers were extremely irresponsible to lend massively to Third World countries, thereby plunging them into debt (17 words).

7.2.D   **1** **1** d   **2** f   **3** j   **4** e   **5** h   **6** g   **7** b   **8** i   **9** a   **10** c.

2
1 repayment	**2** extension	**3** purchase	**4** reaping
5 acquisition	**6** discussion	**7** avoidance	**8** variation
9 agreement	**10** promise	**11** backing	**12** failure
13 seizure	**14** requirement	**15** negotiation	**16** sale
17 distribution	**18** division	**19** lease	**20** ownership
21 expectation	**22** specification	**23** earnings	**24** rating.

3 **1** failure   **2** backing   **3** division
      4 negotiations/discussions   **5** extension   **6** repayment
      7 sale   **8** earnings   **9** agreement.

UNIT 8

8.1.B   **1** b   **2** e   **3** h   **4** f   **5** j   **6** k   **7** g   **8** i   **9** d
               10 l   **11** c   **12** a   **13** m   **14** n   **15** o.

8.1.C   *Suggested answers*
1 Institutional investors; insurance companies; pension funds; mutual funds; bank trust departments
Commodities: petroleum; gold; coffee beans; pork bellies.
Blue-chip stocks: American Express; BASF; De Beers; Eastman Kodak; Nestlé; Sony
Real estate: a vacant plot of land; an office block; a factory; a condominium.
3 John McGregor may want to buy and furnish a house in two years' time; he should therefore choose an investment which doesn't carry too much risk and which is fairly liquid. I would recommend . . .
I would say that Mrs Davies's main concern is to receive a steady income without taking undue risk. I would advise her to . . .
Mr Black can probably afford to take on some risk as he has a good steady income and some capital already invested in real estate. I think the best solution . . .
If Mrs Dangerfield has enough capital now to buy some real estate in Miami then she should do so. If not, I suggest . . .
A rise in copper prices in, say, six months' time would be bad for Mrs Leclerc's business. She might therefore consider . . .

8.2.A   **The Commodities Exchange Center, New York (tapescript)**
Welcome to the Commodities Exchange Center. The CEC functions on behalf of the four independent exchanges that trade here. They are: the Coffee, Sugar and Cocoa Exchange, COMEX, the New York Cotton Exchange and the New York Mercantile Exchange. Each of these exchanges trades in a variety of different futures and options contracts. Small maps on the windows in front of you show where the various trading rings of each exchange are located.
     The trading floor, of course, is where the action takes place. What you're seeing here, is the law of supply and demand freely at work in an open marketplace. What looks like chaos is actually a highly organised process of trading in futures contracts and in options on futures.
     Like an auction the futures market assures both buyer and seller of the prevailing price at any point in time. This process of price discovery is one of the market's two major economic functions. The other is the shifting of risk from hedgers to speculators.
     Hedgers represent commercial interests – such as producers, dealers or processors – whose business involves the sale or purchase of the actual commodity. They enter the futures market in order to protect themselves from major fluctuations in the cash price of commodities they plan to buy or sell in the future. Speculators, on the other hand, are investors who are willing to assume the price risks that hedgers want to avoid. They're willing partly because futures contracts are highly leveraged investments and an initially small amount of risk capital – called a margin deposit – can result in a sizeable profit or loss as market prices rise and fall. Speculators add liquidity to the market, and help keep prices competitive although they generally have little interest in possession of the commodity itself. The basic unit of every trade is the futures contract. It specifies the quantity, quality, and month of delivery of a particular commodity. The price of each contract is determined by open outcry between buyer and seller when the contract is traded.
     Traditionally, futures contracts have been traded on specific physical commodities. These include agricultural commodities like coffee, sugar, cotton or orange juice, metals, such as gold, silver, copper or platinum, and energy products, like gasoline or crude oil. More recently, a number of financial futures have been introduced on the US dollar index,

or the consumer price index, for example. Contracts in all four categories – agriculture, metals, energy, and financial futures – are traded here at the Commodities Exchange Center and new contracts are introduced from time to time. In an open marketplace, nothing is quite as constant as change.

In addition to the futures contracts themselves options are traded here too. Very briefly, an option on a futures contract conveys the right – but not the obligation – to either buy or sell – depending on the kind of option held – a specific futures contract at a specific price during a specified period of time. Options provide additional trading opportunities for commercial market participants and an alternative approach for the individual investor.

As you look at the trading floor, you can see many of the elements of a futures transaction taking place. Let's start with the phone clerks – they're the people you see at telephone and teletype stations all around the floor.

A trade is initiated when a customer somewhere in the world calls his commodity broker with an order to buy or sell. The broker transmits that order to the trading floor by teletype or telephone. The phone clerk writes the order on an order ticket – time stamps it to record the exact time it was received – then gives it to a runner, who takes it to a floor broker at the appropriate trading ring – the only place where trading can legally occur.

There, the broker executes the order by open outcry, as required by the rules of the exchange so that everyone present can bid or offer and will know the details of each new transaction. Of course when everyone's shouting, it's sometimes hard to hear, so the brokers also use hand signals – palm in to buy, palm out to sell.

Once the trade is made, the floor broker notes the details on the order ticket and on his trading card. A runner returns the order ticket to the phone clerk who time stamps it again and then reports the execution of the trade back to the broker who initiated the order. He then notifies his client.

At the trading ring, floor reporters employed by the respective exchanges use hand signals to relay the prices of all new trades to recording clerks, stationed in a rostrum near each ring. The recording clerks enter all new prices into the CEC's central computer system. Within seconds, the large electronic display boards all around the sides of the trading floor are automatically updated with the latest price information. Simultaneously, the same information is relayed to video display terminals and newswire services throughout the world. Still the trade isn't quite complete.

Back at the trading ring, clerks collect the floor brokers' trading cards periodically, and report the trades to the clearing association for that exchange. There, computers match the buyer and seller for each trade, and any breaks – or unmatched trades – are resolved. At this point, the clearing association assumes the role of opposite party to every transaction as the buyer to every seller and the seller to every buyer. At the end of each business day, the clearing association balances the accounts of each of its members.

Futures trading is an exciting, dynamic process, offering the savvy investor an opportunity for highly leveraged profits, providing commercial interest with protection against major price fluctuations and benefiting individual consumers with more stable, competitive prices for the things they buy.

What you're watching is a major part of the world economy at work.

The display panels above the windows and near the door will tell you more about the activities here at the Commodities Exchange Center.

For more information about trading in futures or options, contact one of the individual exchanges.

Thank you.

1 Coffee, Sugar and Cocoa Exchange; COMEX (Commodities Exchange); New York Cotton Exchange; New York Mercantile Exchange.
2 On the trading floor.
3 Shifting risk from hedgers to speculators.
4 Representatives of commercial interest producers, dealers, processors.
5 No. Futures contracts are highly leveraged investments.
6 No. He is generally interested in trading the contract (not the commodity itself) at a profit.
7 By open outcry between buyer and seller, as at any auction.
8 US dollar index and consumer price index.
9 The right (but not the obligation) to either buy or sell a specific futures contract at a specific price during a specific period of time.
10 They shout and use hand signals.
11 Electronic display boards; video display terminals; newswire services.
Grid:
Customer calls commodity broker (CB) with order to buy or sell; CB transmits the order to the trading floor; phone clerk (PC) writes the order on an order ticket; runner (R) takes order to a floor broker (FB) at the appropriate trading ring; FB executes the order by open outcry; FB notes the details of the trade; R returns order ticket to PC; PC stamps ticket again; PC reports execution of trade back to CB; CB notifies client.

8.2.E

Yesterday's trading at the London Stock Exchange (tapesricpt)
Yesterday's stock market trading saw investors taking a subdued view of prospects for the short-term. With Wall Street looking less confident following last week's US employment data, UK equities spent most of the session on the downside and closed 15.4 points lower on the FT-SE scale at 2,519.9.

Strategists at several leading securities firms suggested that although prospects for a further rise in UK equities before the year-end were still good, the next few months might prove less certain. Some lines of good quality stocks were on offer, suggesting that fund managers are reshaping portfolios.

However, sterling's continued firmness against the German mark raised hopes of a further cut in UK base rates, all the more so as the latest UK retail price index is confidently expected to show a significant fall in domestic inflation.

For much of the day, the equity market was led by activity in the stock index futures sector.

At worst, the FTSE was 25.3 points down before the market rallied, ignoring the early fall at Wall Street where the Dow Jones had fallen 6 points.

City traders maintained that the day had not been particularly busy; it was certainly well down on last week's hectic trading.

Suggested answers
Wall Street: looking less confident
US employment data; not good (implied)
UK equities yesterday: closed 15.4 points down
UK equities in the short-term: prospects uncertain
Fund managers: reshaping portfolios
Sterling; continued firmness against the German mark
UK base rates; hopes of a further cut
UK retail price index; expected to show fall in inflation
Footsie: dropped 25.3 points before the market rallied
Yesterday's trading: not particularly busy.

8.2.F

1 but; so
2 as/as soon as; so as
3 as/as soon as; although
4 Despite; which
5 subsequently; before
6 During; because/as
7 By the time; Nevertheless
8 Prior to; In addition

UNIT 9
9.1.A

1 Financial accounting is for outside use whereas management accounting is for internal use.
Public accountants (chartered accountants) are responsible for financial accounting (eg auditing the company's financial statements). Private accountants are concerned with management accounting (eg generating and interpreting financial reports).
A controller has a top-level position and is responsible for monitoring and cross-checking financial data. A book-keeper has a more routine position and is responsible for recording financial transactions.
Assets are what a company owns. Liabilities are what a company owes and are claims against the company's assets.
The P & L account is a summary of the company's past transactions. The cash-flow forecast is a projection of the company's future activities.
2 1 c 2 h 3 a 4 f 5 b 6 i 7 e 8 d 9 g 10 j.
3 a net sales minus cost of goods sold
  b gross profit minus total operating expenses
  c net income plus other income and minus other expenses
  d pre-tax profits minus income taxes
  e sum of total current assets, total fixed assets and total intangible assets
  f common stock plus retained earnings.

9.1.B

1 e   2 a   3 b   4 j   5 n   6 f   7 l   8 m   9 g
10 k   11 p   12 c   13 h   14 o   15 i   16 d.

9.1.C

Calypso Potteries plc	
Current assets **13 3 16 11**	Current liabilities **8 15 4**
Fixed assets **1 10 7 12**	Long-term liabilities **5**
Intangible assets **2 14 9**	Shareholders equity **6**

9.1.D

BALANCE SHEET (US LAYOUT)

ASSETS

Current Assets
Cash		100,00	
Ending merchandise		300,000	
Accounts receivable		250,000	
TOTAL CURRENT ASSETS			650,000

Fixed assets
Equipment		1,000,000	
Building and land		2,000,000	
TOTAL FIXED ASSETS			3,000,000
TOTAL ASSETS			**3,650,000**

LIABILITIES AND SHAREHOLDERS' EQUITY

Current liabilities
Accounts payable	200,000		
Accrued wages payable	100,000		
TOTAL CURRENT LIABILITIES		300,000	

Long term liabilities
Mortgage on building and land		1,500,000	
TOTAL LIABILITIES			1,800,000

Shareholders' Equity
Owners' equity		375,000	
Retained earnings		1,475,000	
TOTAL SHAREHOLDERS' EQUITY			1,850,000
TOTAL LIABILITIES AND SHAREHOLDERS' EQUITY			**3,650,000**

INCOME STATEMENT (US LAYOUT)

REVENUES
Gross sales		2,000,000	
Less returns and discounts		50,000	
NET SALES			1,950,000

COST OF GOODS SOLD
Beginning inventory		200,000	
Purchases	1,400,000		
Less: purchase discounts	200,000	1,200,000	
NET PURCHASES		1,400,000	
Cost of goods available for sale		300,000	1,100,000
Less: ending inventory			850,000
COST OF GOODS SOLD			

GROSS PROFIT
Operating expenses			
Selling expenses	200,000		
Advertising expenses	400,000	600,000	
TOTAL OPERATING EXPENSES			
General expenses			
Office supplies	25,000		
General admin. expenses	200,000	225,000	825,000
TOTAL GENERAL EXPENSES			25,000
TOTAL OPERATING EXPENSES			0
NET INCOME			25,000
Other income and expenses			0
Pre-tax profit			25,000
Income taxes			
NET PROFIT			

9.2.A

Summary 1: there is no reference; the writer fails to document his source.
Summary 2: even though the source is documented, the writer should have used direct quotes for the phrase taken word for word from the original.
Summary 3: perfect.
Summary 4: the writer gives the impression that only the phrase quoted belongs to the original author while the ideas in the text are the writer's own.
Summary 5: the writer has interpreted the original author's ideas wrongly and has attributed the interpretation to the author.

9.2.B

Suggested answer
A company's profitability is only meaningful if related to the level of equity invested in the company. This ratio, or 'rate of return on investment' is a more important indicator than increased sales volume, especially in the long-run, Effective use of capital leads to good returns, which leads to real growth, thus attracting more capital. Ineffective use of capital has an opposite effect. (64 words)

9.2.C

1		
1 spotted	2 withdraw	3 to allocate
4 tie up	5 would affect/affected	6 recorded/incurred
7 designed	8 been mounting up	9 owe
10 to forecast	11 to carry out/provide	12 depreciate
13 carried out	14 to record/classify.	

2		
1 a record	2 a classification	3 a presentation
4 an evaluation	5 a performance	6 a loan
7 a regulation	8 an allocation	9 a generation
10 an interpretation	11 a simplification	12 a conversion
13 a withdrawal	14 a payment	15 a deduction
16 a depreciation	17 an appearance	18 a summary
19 a subtraction	20 a projection	21 a statement
22 an involvement	23 a calculation	24 a capitalisation.

3		
1 summary	2 statement	3 performance
4 regulations	5 generation	6 depreciation
7 projection	8 allocation	9 simplification
10 record.		

9.2.D

1 k	2 i	3 b	4 l	5 g	6 c	7 o	8 n
9 m	10 a	11 d	12 j	13 h	14 e	15 f	16 p.

9.3.A

1

	Problem	Excuse given	Resolution of problem
Conversation 1	Wrong prices on invoice	Computer error	Will send new invoice immediately
Conversation 2	Invoice received but no goods	Keyboard error and clerical slip-up	Disregard invoice
Conversation 3	Goods received but wrong colour	Misunderstanding due to bad telephone line	Send it back at supplier's cost and ship new consignment today
Conversation 4	Unauthorised overdraft	Cheque mislaid in post	Send a new cheque
Conversation 5	Non-receipt of foreign currency transfer	Staff shortage in central office	Will arrange transfer immediately

Complaints, apologies and excuses (tapescript)
Conversation 1:
Janet Groves: Hello, is that Mr Thomas?
Mr Thomas: Yes, speaking
JG: Oh hello. This is Janet Groves from Parker and Parker. We've just received a shipment of six office chairs and the prices on the invoice aren't the same as those quoted in your catalogue.
Mr T: Oh dear. Which model was that for, please?
JG: It's . . ., wait a minute, let me just check. Yes. It's model NB 277 and you've got it down in your catalogue at £83 each, but on the invoice you've charged us £88.

Mr T:	£88 is the old price. Our computer people must have forgotten to update it. I'm terribly sorry about that. Anyway, I'm glad you pointed it out to us.
JG:	Oh, that's all right.
Mr T:	Look, I'll get our accounts people to send you out a new invoice immediately. You should receive it by Wednesday at the latest.
JG:	Thank you very much. Goodbye.

Conversation 2:

John Barker:	Hello, John Barker here from Greystoke sportswear. I'd like to speak to someone from your accounts department.
JG:	This is John Gilbert, Accounts, speaking. What can I do for you Mr Barker?
JB:	Your people have just sent us a bill for four dozen children's teeshirts which we'd never even ordered and never received. You know, this isn't the first time we've had trouble with your people.
JG:	Well I'm sorry to hear you say that, Mr Barker. Do you think you could give me the reference number on your invoice?
JB:	Which one's that? 4027927 is that the one?
JG:	No sir, that's the telephone number. The reference number is in the top left-hand corner of the invoice.
JB:	Top left-hand corner. Oh yeah, here it is. 73737 AJ.
JG:	Right thank you. If you'd just like to hold the line for a few moments I'll just check that out. *(pause)* Ah yes, here it is. 73737 AJ. Four dozen model 37 P, mixed sizes. Which company did you say you were?
JB:	Greystoke. Greystoke Sportswear of Llanelly.
JG:	I'm afraid there must have been a clerical slip-up or a keyboard error. This order was for a store in Bicester.
JB:	Well. I suppose mistakes do happen.
JG:	Yes, I'm afraid they do occasionally. If I could just ask you to disregard the invoice and accept our apologies for the inconvenience this has caused you.

Conversation 3:

Betty Miller:	Hello, is that the Sales Department?
Jack Ladd:	Yes it is. May I help you?
BM:	This is Betty Miller speaking, from Sacha's in the Strand. We ordered five dozen tubes of cherry lipstick and you've sent us the wrong colour. I don't know what colour it is but it's definitely not cherry.
JL:	Could you hold on a moment. Please, I'll just find the order form. *(pause)* Did you phone this order through or was it faxed?
BM:	I phoned it through personally.
JL:	Oh well, I'm afraid there must have been a misunderstanding. Maybe it was a bad line. The person who took your order wrote down 'berry' instead of 'cherry'.
BM:	Actually I remember the line was bad that day. It sounded as though somebody was frying bacon and eggs. But I did spell it out.
JL:	I do apologise. If you'd like to send back the consignment, we'll refund the postage. I'll get a new order down to the warehouse straight away. You should receive it within 48 hours. Is that all right?

Conservation 4:

John Owen:	Hello, may I speak to Mr Jason Humphrey, please?
Jason Humphrey:	Speaking.
JO:	Hello, Mr Humphrey. This is John Owen of Western Bank speaking. I'm calling you because of a small problem that has just come to our attention.
JH:	Oh? What is that?
JO:	Well. I'm afraid that you've greatly exceeded your authorised overdraft facility and your account is currently in the red to the tune of £2,140.
JH:	But that's impossible! I sent you a cheque from my Building Society account over 10 days ago. It was for £2,200. I've got the cheque stub right here.
JO:	Well we don't seem to have received your cheque. Do you know if your Building Society account has been debited?
JH:	No, I'm afraid I don't.
JO:	Well I think the best thing would be to find out if they've debited your account and if they haven't it means that the cheque must have got mislaid in the post.
JH:	Yes. And it won't have been the first time. Anyway, I'll check with my Building Society straight away and if my account hasn't been debited I'll cancel the first cheque and bring you over a new one first thing this afternoon. Would that be OK?
JO:	Yes, certainly.

Conversation 5:

Marilyn Fletcher:	Hello, is that Mr Whitehouse? This is Marilyn Fletcher speaking.
Peter Whitehouse:	Ah, good afternoon Miss Fletcher.
MF:	I'm calling you because one of our agents has just faxed us from Washington to say that the foreign currency transfer hasn't come through yet. It's been almost 24 hours since I asked you.
PW:	I do apologise, Miss Fletcher, but we've got a major staff shortage over at central office; apparently three-quarters of the FOREX division have gone down with some mysterious bug.
MF:	Yes, but this is urgent, Mr Whitehouse. Can't you do something?
PW:	Yes, of course, I'll arrange the transfer myself, immediately.
MF:	I'd be so grateful if you could.

9.3.B

1 The size of the order is so large thatt Regal Leather's production capacity would be saturated during the months of June, July and August. This may lead to a disruption in supplies to other (regular) customers.
Western Emporium is a new customer. Its credit worthiness would have to be checked carefully and appropriate guarantees made.
Payment will not be made until November 1 1993. This would present Regal Leather with a serious cash flow deficit.

2

Regal Leather: Cash flow forecast						
	June	July	August	Sept	Oct	Nov
Receipts	155,000	40,000	0	0	0	505,000
Payments	135,000	135,000	135,000	63,000	123,000	123,000
Receipts +/– payments	20,000	(95,000)	(135,000)	(63,000)	(123,000)	382,000
Opening balance	45,000	65,000	(30,000)	(165,000)	(228,000)	(351,000)
Closing balance	65,000	(30,000)	(165,000)	(228,000)	(351,000)	31,000

3 The dilemma is to find a way of accepting a profitable order without running up a huge cash flow deficit which would jeopardise the company's financial heath. Many solutions may be envisaged:
   ● taking out a loan (ask students to calulate cost at current rates of interest; would costs be prohibitive?)
   ● negotiating with Western Emporium for better terms (shorter payment period, higher price, reduction of order, etc)
   ● negotiating with suppliers for better conditions
   ● negotiating with workforce for deferred overtime payment etc.

**Company focus:
Financial services at
Merrill Lynch**

1 Longer life expectancy therefore greater demand for comfortable retirement; importance of financing eductation, etc; baby boomers represent huge market.
Merrill Lynch is widespread, offers skilled consultancy, superior products and educational back-up.
2 Very important because (a) fastest growing sector in US economy and (b) created over 90% of new jobs in 1991.
Merrill Lynch offers: cash management; financing and retirement planning; evaluation of mature business and development of disposal plans; equity, mezzanine and senior financing; working capital management.
3 Trends: enormous global capital market surge; US stock market boom; plummeting interest rates; boom in debt and equity financing; slowdown in mergers and acquisitions.
Merrill Lynch continued to advise clients on acquisitions, divestitures, joint ventures, etc in spite of reduced activity in these areas.
4 Liberalised cross-border trade and heightened global competition have forced governments to help their economies become more competitive.
5 Merrill Lynch can help states and municipalities solve their funding needs by helping them raise capital.